THE
LAST CIGARETTE
ON EARTH

—A BOOK OF POEMS—

THE
LAST CIGARETTE
ON EARTH

—A BOOK OF POEMS—

BENJAMIN ALIRE SÁENZ

CINCO PUNTOS PRESS
WWW.CINCOPUNTOS.COM

FIRST EDITION
10 9 8 7 6 5 4 3 2 1

Library of Congress Cataloging-in-Publication Data

Names: Sáenz, Benjamin Alire, author.
Title: The last cigarette on earth : a book of poems / by Benjamin Alire Sáenz.
Description: First edition. | El Paso, Texas : Cinco Puntos Press, 2017.
Identifiers: LCCN 2016059370 | ISBN 9781941026656 (paperback : alk. paper)
Subjects: | BISAC: POETRY / American / Hispanic American.
Classification: LCC PS3569.A27 A6 2017 | DDC 811/.54--dc23
LC record available at https://lccn.loc.gov/2016059370

Book and cover design/illustration by Antonio Castro H.

for Carlos

When I see the rain falling on the desert,
I think of you.

PROLOGUE: WORD

There is something
perfect about the day.

He has been on a long journey, traveling

by night
always living in the shadows

hoping to find the missing pieces
of himself. He wants
to build himself into a home.

He took too many detours, chasing the dragon
and every rat
that crossed his path
chasing them into the sewers.

He almost drowned there. In the sewer. With all the rats.

Now, he is resting
from the futile search that has left
him empty and exhausted.
He lives now in a disquieting
aftermath.
He wants his mind to be
clear as the morning sky
after a rain.

He wants to speak
with a voice as soft as a tender leaf.

He wants to remember
                    and understand the crooked roads

he has walked. He will step into the landscapes

where he lost and broke himself.   He saw miles
                                        of perfect lawns
but when he stepped
                                    discovered weeds
and stickers everywhere
his clothes torn
his feet bleeding
                                        his idiot tongue
                                        cursing the ground.

He wants to gather all the lost selves
                        scattered across the fields

                                    and piece them together
like the pieces of the puzzles
he played with as a boy.

                                He has lost
himself

so many times that he wonders how

he still finds himself
                            in one piece. But
he is *not* in one piece.
All the king's horses and all the king's men couldn't—

He is thinking that he is still here, breathing,
                                            a miracle
though he does not believe in miracles.

He is thinking of his mother's face, the soft in her eyes,

                        how she lived her days
wearing a look of gratitude and grace.

Forgiveness was a weight she carried without complaint.

He wants now

                        the weight of a love
                        instead of the debris
                        of nights too well remembered.

He does not know
        which direction to take so he might arrive—

Like a fishhook, there are words caught
                                in his throat.

He wants to cast out those words into the morning light

and watch them disappear into the desert's dusk.

Only then will he be free, with the knowledge
                        that what   was once   caught

in his throat   has found a place to live.

It eluded us then, but that's no matter—tomorrow we will run faster, stretch out our arms farther. . . . And one fine morning—

—F. Scott Fitzgerald

He

He has misspent a lifetime looking for himself.

Last Night Another Dream

Another road. Again it is night. All
there is: the walking and the walking and the walking.

The weary legs and the weary mind. He follows a long line
of people marching in front of him. The masses move with

a humility he does not possess. Or perhaps he possessed it once but
lost it as if were a wallet or a credit card or the keys to his truck. He

is a careless man who has lived a careless life. Still he follows

this useless procession of pilgrims in a world that no longer
has a church, a world that has no saints to guide them towards

salvation. No candles left to light the dark. The saints
have gone away. The saints have been disappeared. Or perhaps

they live in exile. Or perhaps they were hunted down, killed
on a quiet night. The last saint died alone. In the desert. She was

crossing a border as she felt the bullet pierce her heart. Her last
image was of a fair-skinned man with eyes as blue as the sea

who was raising his gun and dancing victoriously in the light
of a dying sun. That is what he is thinking. The man. He

is making all these stories up in his head. He does not know
why. The stories come to him. He does not know how to stop

the stories from coming. The man who does not even feel

himself to be a man. He wonders where the feelings and sensations
of his body have gone. To live with the last, dead saint.

Now, he is crossing the bridge to the other side. He is tired
of crossing bridges over and over and over again. He is drowning

in an ocean of people washing themselves in their own blood. Then

suddenly he finds himself

walking through the spent fields in the Valley of Juárez. There
are no trees left to bathe the sands in shade, no trees to catch

the sound of the slight breezes. He watches the new sun
rising but there is no new day, no new beginnings, no expectant

lovers waiting for his return. He begins walking on the side
of an isolate road. All the people have gone and the desert

is empty. Again he is alone.

But this does not matter. He is half in love with the word
alone. He does not know where he is. And then *he knows*.

This is the highway to Chihuahua.
In the distance he spies an approaching truck. He watches

himself falling to the ground in a rain of bullets. He begins

to sweat. His panicked lungs *where is the air where is the air?*
The world is made of lead. The world is made of lead.

The black truck speeding closer and closer and closer. He
hears the pounding of his heart—and then he smiles. For

a blessed moment he feels. Something—*something*—even if
that something is a thing called fear. Maybe that is the last

thing a man feels before he dies. Maybe that is what the last
saint felt. He tries to see the face of the last man he kissed. He

thinks of lovers he once had and knows that *lovers* is a serious
word and there was nothing that resembled that word

beneath the surface of all the hands that touched him. He
thinks of the stories he has heard on the radio or read

in newspapers, armless bodies lying on sidewalks with
angry poems pinned to their chests. And for all the sadness

that has lived inside him, he does not want to die. Not
like this. No, not like, not like this. He has learned

the art of shaking himself awake from such dreams.

When he opens his eyes, he finds himself lying

on his bed. He breathes in and out until the trembling
leaves. He is safe. He will stop reading the newspapers, all

of them, will stop thinking of the dead, of the dying, stop
asking the impossible, insipid question *Why?* He curses

the journalists who look for a truth that does not exist.

He curses himself for not knowing what to ask. He curses
the two countries he loves because they are even more

careless than him. The countries he loves, as careless

as Tom and Daisy in *The Great Gatsby*. Tomorrow he will drive
forty-two miles north, away from the border. He will

visit his mother. He will give her the flowers he arranged
in a blue vase. He will memorize her smile as she takes

the vase and breathes in the fragrance of the roses. That is
what he will do—drive to see his mother. He pictures himself

as he puts his queer shoulder to the wheel and makes his way
toward the house of the woman who taught him to laugh.

No one will want to kill him on the road to her house.

Because

Because he does not trust his eyes. Because he believes in art and paintings and black and white photography—the feel of charcoal on his fingers as he rubs it onto the rough paper. Because he believes in the canvas and the paint and the brush. Because he believes in the words he has written and the words he is writing at this very moment more than in the things he sees, believes in them more than he ever believed in the women and the men he touched and loved. Because he has come to understand that seeing is a beautiful and complicated and impossible thing that can never be understood or explained and knows, too, that he cannot even trust his own eyes and must live in his own blindness. Because he has seen too much and felt too much and knows now that he cannot believe in his own body and its deceitful and impossible desires so how can he begin to believe in his own memory? Because he is tired of sitting in front of a screen, his still nimble fingers numb from touching a keyboard for hours on end as if it were a piano banging out sad and angry notes struggling to become a song. Because he is tired of words owning him, telling him what to do, what to say—but the words—the words—one day he will put them together in such a way and form a sentence that will beat like the wings of a bird and in the beating, beating, beating, he will see. He will live.

He walks the city with a camera.

He listens to the sound of his steps on the pavement.

It has been a cold winter.

One cold front has followed another.

Today, hints of green, the afternoon bathed in light again.
He yearns to live on that line where the shadows begin.

He must choose: to be swallowed by the light
or to be swallowed by the shadows of the night.

NIGHT DISAPPEARING INTO A PATIENT SKY
for Michael

Boys reach for things. Not believing
what they see, they have to touch.

Boys are greedy beings. They grow
into men who want to touch the light. Always wanting
what they cannot have.

When he was a boy, God
was the light. He was large, vague, mean. God, his rules
complicated, unknowable. The boy had no patience
for theology. God was everywhere

—but where were his hands?

When he was a boy—now he is
a man. Now he is a man. He is in love

with fire. There is dance in the flames. The dance
resides in the wind. The wind, like the light,
is impossible to touch. He is obsessed with shadows
no fire he builds can touch. He studies the corners
of the room where the light of a burning bulb can
never reach.

There are places in the world
not even the sun can touch.

He loves the light
but loves the darkness too.

Boys reach for things.
They grow into men who want to touch the light,
men who only understand the darkness of the world.

It is his heart that's dark.

Some days, he wakes at dawn
and runs to the window to witness the night
disappearing into the patient sky.

There are places in the ocean
that are dead now. There, in the darkest corners of the earth
the light is banished.

One day, the blue of the sky
will leave in anger. Never to return.

Translating Heidegger

The sudden urge to understand
a difficult passage from Heidegger. The urge becoming
an obsession as he wakes whispering *Dasein*. He thinks
of Tom, his easy laugh, his deep and generous voice.
He envied all Tom's understanding. At twenty, Tom is perfect,
his dark Italian eyes exploding with the secrets of German
philosophy. He pictures himself taking notes as Tom explains,
interprets—four or five of them gathered in his room, idiot
students with so little hunger for knowledge. He is smoking
a cigarette as he listens to Tom's voice and he is thinking
of incense. Tom was a good priest. He explained Descartes
to anyone around him who would listen. But one day

Tom hungered for another kind of knowledge—he looked up
from the pages of a book and saw a woman. All the angels
fell away. *Amo ergo sum*. And him? He could never be
like Tom. He never gave a damn about Descartes. Never gave
a damn about Heidegger—though he liked pronouncing
his name. He's sorry for all his shallowness. For other things
too. He knew he could never be too sorry. He was Catholic
after all. He could never be too sorry.

Now—in his dreams—
there are birds falling from the sky. He has started
to paint all the birds. A friend keeps asking him what
they mean, the birds in his paintings. "They can't fly!
They're just falling!" He can't explain. He's not Karl Jung.
He's not even an art critic—maybe not even a good
painter. Maybe he's just internalized an old Hitchcock movie
that was more or less about desire and sexual repression.

Another phrase slams into his brain: *Jedem das Seine*. He waits
for the translation but it does not arrive. He sees the words
written on the gates of a camp. His abilities as a translator
are not improving. There are many arts he will never
master. Beethoven was deaf. Goya too. There were
monsters in their heads that drove them mad. All
the dazzling darkness of the deaf. But him? His hearing
is fine. What good is that?

  His life has become a series of bad translations.
This means *that*. And that means *this*. This and that
have nothing to do with art. Goya, Beethoven, Heidegger.

All the great translators are themselves untranslatable.

He's thinking of his former lives. He is rummaging through
boxes, tossing out photographs and fragments of the past.
Why did he save this? And this? And this? He finds a box
of bullets. When his father was sick, he bought a gun. His
father wanted to kill. Parkinson's. Doctors. Himself. One day
his father woke shouting and shouting at his mother *¿Dónde está
la pistola?* His brother got rid of the gun. And him? He wound
up with the bullets. What will he do with them—him?—who
never owned a gun? Goya would have known what to do with
the bullets. Beethoven too. He picked onions as a boy.
The stench of rotting onions assaults him in unexpected
moments. Even now after so many years, that stench comes
back to him. He turns, almost expecting to see himself

at thirteen, bending to clip the roots of an onion with steel
scissors that leave his hands callused and angry at the earth.
Ruben eats onions like apples. He has discovered the sweetness
of onions. He envies his friend. His grandmother had
a peach tree. She spent summers chasing away the birds, an art
she never mastered. (Here they are again, the birds). He remembers
thinking that his grandmother would have done anything

to protect her peaches. Yes, she would have shot every last
bird that invaded her tree—except she hated guns. Once
she stared down a cop who kept his gun in his holster
during Mass. *Jesus didn't die, not for that*. Sometimes, he's sorry
he didn't become a farmer. He would have grown acres
of organic tomatoes. He would have paid poor city boys
five cents for every worm they picked off the plants. Boys
should know about worms and tomatoes, how they grow,
the dangers they face, what it costs them to survive as
they ripen into the color of a man's blood. He got lost
on the first day of school. He spent years looking for himself.
He thinks he's finally found at least a fragment of himself
that he can trust. He doesn't dream the devil anymore. When
he was five, the devil was always chasing him. Maybe it was
only Descartes' evil genius. It's true, when he was a boy,
the devil wanted him, his mind, his body, his heart. Perhaps
the devil managed to steal a piece of him—

and has kept it ever since.

Descartes. The devil. And now
there are birds. He doesn't know what all these flecks
and fragments are trying to tell him. Maybe he deserves all
the things that wander in and out of his dreams. Who is
to say what we all deserve? The Nazis knew. Dick Cheney,
he knew. *Dasein*. *¿Dónde está la pistola?* The river is poor and dirty
but water is water. Born in the desert, he came into this
world a thirsty man. He will always love the river. He could
write that in any language the world has ever known. Tom
explaining *Dasein*. Ruben eating an onion. His grandmother
holding a perfect peach. Birds falling from the sky. This is

what life is: an endless stream of memories. When he wakes
from his dreams, he will step into the waters.

TOUCH

In the stillness, he runs
his finger across his lips and trembles. He rises and makes
the bed. He puts on the coffee and pours himself a cup.
He sits down and begins to write:

> *All the damaged boys who grew up*
> *to be damaged men. The boys who were damaged*
> *and poor went on to damage their wives and shoot*
> *birds down from the sky. The damaged boys*
> *of means attended college, became professionals,*
> *versed themselves in the sciences and the finer points*
> *of torture—then learned to call it something else.*
> *It's all about words and how you put them together.*
> *Any politician or two-bit poet can tell you that.*
> *This has nothing to do with meaning or morality.*
> *This is all about aesthetics. This is about hiding*
> *the blood.*

He stares at what he has written. He wonders where
all these strange and violent thoughts come from.
He pictures himself sitting in a chair, his hands
tied. He does not even understand the questions
they are asking him. A man grabs him by the chin
and lifts his face up towards him and says: "We are
going to cut off your balls." He stares back
into the angry face, not caring about the reasons.
Reason does not exist in this room and they can
do what they like with people like him—and they
will casually call it a harsh interrogation tactic.
The men in the room are serious and sincere. They
have no irony in them. They believe this is necessary.

They believe he deserves this. And so he hears
himself tell them: "Go ahead. Go ahead and grab
my balls and cut them off. *Be quick and cut them off.*"
The room is small and dark but large enough
to hold their secrets. No eyes will see. No mouth
will tell. No one will know. They will make him
as damaged as they are—except *they* get to keep
their balls. Oh, yes, how could he forget? He must
tell them something they want to know. His confession
is the most important part of the whole ritual. It's all
so Catholic. He has to use words, reveal information, spit
something out, accuse himself. Accuse others. Where
to begin? There are so many things he could accuse
himself of. But then he hears himself scream out
the words he has been holding:
                                        I hate I hate I hate you.
It sounds almost like a song. Almost like a—but
then he thinks to himself that he has only revealed
what they already know. He wants to laugh and say,
Guess you cut off my balls for nothing. He knows they are
waiting for him to say something else, so he says:
I hate myself too. He is sitting there, facing his interrogators
and he understands that the world belongs to them.
They can have the world and all that's in it. They will
always win. Except they'll never have his love—which
is the only thing they want. They want his love. How
sick is that? The whole world is blind and drowning
itself in the blood of its martyrs. And he begins
to write a speech in his head but this is the only
word that comes to mind: *Freedom.* That is the only
word left on his tongue. It *is* all about aesthetics.
He was once a preacher. He is done with all of that.
Too many nice words were involved. That particular
aesthetic has lost its appeal. He doesn't much care
for holy men. He has stopped going to their churches.
There are too many mean and murderous creatures

living in his heart. Those creatures like to cuss.
They like to scream. The creatures have made a good
home everywhere in his body like a metastasized
cancer. Maybe he likes it that way. Maybe he invited
them in. So what? He still believes in the light.
He laughs: *How's that for a confession?*

He sleeps for days. For weeks.
He has been very sick. No one knows for sure
what is wrong with him. One day, he finally wakes—
and the dawning sun is streaming through his room.
He wants to drown in that river of light. The whole
world is luminous. *God*, he whispers, *it's all so beautiful*.
He sticks out his hands and stares at them. *These are
my hands*. He thinks that it would be so beautiful
to touch someone like the morning light is running
its fingers through his room. To touch someone. Not
to hurt, not to torture. But to take his own trembling
hands and touch another man's hands
                    in a wordless and untortured moment.

The Tree He Is Painting

The sky is calm and blue and cold. The leafless tree is still. Waiting for spring, waiting to bloom again. Spending his days gathering coins, the man walks into the store and buys cigarettes and beer. Nothing can rid him of his thirst. Nothing can rid him of his hunger. The woman knocking at the door wants to know how much he pays for rent. Too much she says *has de ser un hombre rico*. He misses the sound of someone breathing next to him in his bed. The divorce was his idea. He deserves what he got—and didn't get—and never got. This is the season of want. He's refraining from calling his former therapist. What would he tell him? *Hi. What's new? I'm fine, I'm fine. You?* It's winter. It's cold outside. He is stir crazy and wishes it was warm enough to open all the windows. Stir crazy is normal for a guy like him. Like a cat that needs to go outside, go hunting. It doesn't matter that the cat is safe and well fed. He needs to go on being a cat. Skulk around, feast on an unsuspecting bird. Poor goddamned bird. The cat needs to be a cat. And him? He needs to go on being a man. What are the rules for that? It's easier being a cat. It's easier being a leafless tree. The novel is almost finished. The story is about a young man who has a therapist. What the young man really wants is a dog, but he doesn't want anyone to ask him where he got the dog idea. Then he would have to talk about his life. He doesn't want to think about the young man he is writing about so he decides to paint a tree. The sky makes him cold. He's thinking that the tree is dreaming a leaf falling from the sky. The tree is leaning out to catch it. All artists ever do is recount their own stories. Some hide this fact better than others. In the mind of every artist, the leaf means something different. A single leaf can't save a tree. He had another dream last night. In the dream it becomes obvious to the dreamer that he hasn't learned a damn thing. In the dream he was going to do something *he* knew would end in disaster. And he was still—the *him* in his dream—contemplating doing it, doing what would end in disaster. And he kept whispering *don't do it don't do it*. When he woke, he was tired. The room was cold and he thought for a moment that he would like to sleep the day away. But the boy that once lived inside him had long since abandoned him. The day was more or less normal. The men outside, who gather like a flock of crows around a bottle, were threatening to kill each other. One of them was swinging a board like a bat. He listened to the news on the radio. Israel was bombing the hell out of Gaza. Bombs into Israel. Bombs into Gaza. He is fucking sick of all the killing. He doesn't give a damn anymore whose God anyone believes in. Wouldn't it be lovely to worship human beings? Then there would be no reason to kill, to punish, to torture, no reason to make another woman, another man suffer a world without tenderness.

The leafless tree he is painting is as still as death. It will soon become collateral damage. Who gives a common sparrow about a tree that got in the way of a bomb? They will be forced to repeat what happened in Europe after the war. They will do it again—plant the trees in rows and pretend nothing ever happened, pretend no one died, forget about the bodies buried beneath the foundations of the new cities. The landscape will look neat and sweet as if it were a human invention. The trees will look like tamed crops, poems in iambic pentameter. Four seasons in a year. How many seasons in the life of a tree or a man or a bird or a cat or a drunk or a marriage or a nation? Soon there will be only one season. And then he whispers: *We will call the season drought*. He does not know what the spring will bring. He does not know if it will ever return again.

He wonders if the tree will miss him when he's gone.

A Boy. A Hand. A Bird. A Man.

Some mornings, as he placed his feet on the floor,

He would search the room, almost expecting

A dead bird to be lying at the foot of his bed

Its eyes still open and alive with accusation.

He wants to know how this began, this obsession

With dead birds. Why not dream of birds

That sing and fly? When he was a boy, a bird

Was a bird, each kind was indistinguishable

From another. He was a boy. A boy was a boy. A bird

Was a bird. Birds and trees and a blue sky and a soft

Earth beneath his bare and tender feet. What do boys

Know? Now: dying birds falling from the sky.

In one dream, he was trying to catch all the birds.

But it was no good. All he could do was cry. He wanted

To be done with it, this business of birds and their

Dying. Inexplicably, he wanted it to go on forever.

This was not an obsession. This was a sickness. In one

Of his former lives, while walking a dog he loved,

A grey and common dove with a broken wing

Was flapping for its life in the middle of the street,

Her mate dancing around her as if to will her

To fly. Perhaps it was a dance of goodbye. Perhaps

It was all a ritual of grief. The dog, being a dog

Wanted nothing more than to devour the bird.

He pulled the dog away and left the bird to die—but

Hoped, somehow, that it would live. He cursed himself

When he returned, the dove dead on the street. That

Was when the dreams began.

※

Last night, another dream. There was a boy

Shouting at the sky *Can't you see them! Everywhere, birds*

Are falling from the sky! Look! See! It's you! It's me!

Everyone! We're dying!

He is thinking about torture,

About the systematic ways we can conjure hate

And punish in the name of a god or in the name

Of a nation or in the name of all the dead. Living

Had turned them all into magicians. All the truths

Are darker than anyone cared to think about.

Why think about what's done? What's done

Is done. Why mourn for the water that has found its

Way to the sea? And who really gives a damn about

The reflected life? He is thinking about a human hand.

A hand is a thing that can touch, a part of the body

That can torture, that can kill. The tortured men

Had once been boys. Boys like him. A bird

Is a bird. A man is a man. A hand is a hand. He wants

To know when all the boys will be set free.

Night

Again this night, he is thinking of the stars, how he
studied them when he was ten. He hears a voice
in the room. Someone is singing a song. He is in love
with his voice. What would the song look like if
he could see it? Would his song look like sparrows, newly
born, learning to fly in the spring? Swallows scattering
in different directions? Geese flying in perfect formation?
Would a lonely voice look like a man walking through
a dark alley, searching for something to eat or another
man to love. Hunger is everywhere, that's what makes
a singer want to sing. Hunger. He can't remember the last
time he took an hour to lift his head up in wonder at
the night sky. He is too much in love with the azure
of the day. As if the sun was kind. Look what it did to
Icarus. Hunger. That is what makes an artist take a brush
and force his vision on the canvas, or on a wall
or on a scrap piece of paper. If an artist has seen night—
then he has to paint it. Night drives artists insane.
Just ask Van Gogh. Just ask Velázquez. Just ask Siqueiros.
Maybe when you've gone blind or mad, all that's left
to do is dive into the dark. Any decent singer
knows about the night. He is wondering if everyone
in the world is doing what they were meant to do.
How would anyone know? He'd had a lot of jobs
in his life. His body carried his own history of work.
He'd always found a way to feed himself. Hunger
turns them all into workers, makes them immigrants
and travelers. Everyone is walking down a road,
emigres who have lost their faith—but not their hope. Not
their feet either. What good was hope without a good
pair of feet? Sometimes there is so much starvation

that no one gives a damn that the road ends in catastrophe.
No dreams left except the need for food to continue
living just another goddamned day. Every day: beans
and rice and some days the dream of an avocado or
a piece of meat. Or a small cup of rainwater. On a plane
to San Antonio, he vows to go out into the desert
and get drunk on the harsh light of the heavens. He wants
to escape the pollution of light that permeates the city,
the light that seeps into his apartment. Last night,
he woke at 3:40 in the morning. He was disgusted
at all the light in the room, light from the monitor
of his printer, light flooding in from the window,
the lamppost on the corner serving as a full moon
that never wanes. What ever happened to the dark?
He walks into the kitchen, the light on the clock
of Mr. Coffee assaulting him. Night has become nothing
more than a metaphor. There is no real darkness—save
the darkness of the heart. Maybe that's darkness
enough. Joseph Conrad got it right. Was he doing
what he was meant to do or did he force the issue? Maybe
he was supposed to become an architect. Or a therapist.
Or a physicist. Or a singer who breaks people's hearts. Yes.
He is in love with the singer's voice. Once, he wrote
a poem about becoming an eschatologist. He's since
decided that sooner or later, everyone becomes
an eschatologist, regardless of what they've spent
their lives doing between the hours of nine and five. What
does it mean to work? He knows how to pick cotton, pick
onions, pick tomatoes. He knows how to stretch a canvas.
That's work. He knows that night is night. One summer,
his eyes were luminous as he stood under a Tanzanian sky
on fire with the stars—and he was ten again. Ten! He is
frantically brushing the blue pigment onto the canvas.
      He is a mad man painting the night.

Sunday Morning

He drinks a glass of water.
The day is like wide water, without sound. He goes back to bed. He
waits for the light of the new day to enter the room. Bathing
in the old chaos of the sun. When he was a boy his mother told
him not to look into the sun because he would go blind. He
says the word in Spanish *ciego*. He likes the sound of the word
and hears his mother's warning in his original language. He
looked at the sun anyway. Masturbation was like the sun. It was
supposed to make him go blind too. But here he is, his sight
intact. He has never worn sunglasses. When the desert light
hurts his eyes, he bears the pain of it. The word *dolor* arrives
on his lips. He thinks of Michelangelo's Pietà. The word is Italian
for pity. The word is related to compassion.

He hears the bells
of the Cathedral. He will never be free of the Catholic Bells.
He thinks of the poem by William Carlos Williams. How easy
for him to write that poem when he wasn't Catholic. When you
were a Catholic, it was too painful to write about a crucified
God. This is what he is thinking: *I will always be a Catholic but
never be a Catholic again.*

He rises, sits on the bed, studies the light. He is painting
a small mural on the wall. He doesn't like it. Unfinished, already
it is too crowded. He will paint over it and start again. *And
start again.* Life is a pentimento. *Pentimento* is the title of Lillian
Hellman's memoir. She was Dashiell Hammett's lover. Hammett
had left-wing sympathies. He, too, has left-wing sympathies.
Everything is connected.

He stares at the charcoal sketch he is working
on. He likes the simplicity of it. One cup on a table. Another
cup falls off the edge of the page. He is finished with
the sketch. He will work on the background. He thinks of what
the background will be. He likes putting words in his drawings. A
real artist doesn't need words—except if he wants to talk. Some
days he wants to run away from all the words that drench
him like an afternoon downpour in the desert. But there are
other days he wishes all the words in the world could love him
as much as he loved them. He would like to take words
and build a man. And make love to him.

He thinks of going to Starbuck's to buy the Sunday
New York Times. He looks for his shoes. But then he thinks
that today it would be good to send the news away. He thinks
late coffee and oranges in a sunny chair. He knows he cannot shut
out the world. But today he wants to rest from it. He thinks
that everybody needs a day off from the truth. He knows he has
been too much in love with the fight. But he wants something
different now. He puts on some music and listens to Dusty
Springfield. She is singing *Just a little lovin' early in the mornin'*.
He drinks his coffee and sings. Love songs don't make him
feel lonely. Not even sad ones. Finally, he has come to know
that no one has to be in the room for him to love. Sometimes
a warm body wouldn't be such a bad thing. On the other hand
there's that old Mexican saying: *Mejor solo que mal acompañado*.

He thinks of his mother
who is eighty-three. He pictures her getting ready for Mass,
pictures the altar she has in her bedroom. He thinks of his
father who is dead. He wonders if there is a heaven. He still
wonders things like that. He is no different than any boy
remembering what it was like to be loved.

He thinks of his younger sister. He found an old
picture of her. Her first communion, white dress, white veil. Her

bangs are crooked. She cut her own bangs, didn't let their mother comb her hair. She didn't want to be a sweet compliant girl. He pictures his mother talking to her: *No me dejaste peinarte*. She was like that. She is still like that. He is happy because he loves his sister. Some men have sisters they don't love. He has two. He loves them both. They are kind. They are generous. They have their troubles. And they understand what it means to love.

He thinks of all the work he has ahead of him. Dusty Springfield is still singing *when I fell into your open arms*...and there is more coffee in the pot and the bells of the Cathedral are ringing. Today, God and work can wait.

On the Absence of Leaves

Trees are the road to heaven. Climb them. Something
he wrote in a notebook years ago, when words
were sweet as summer apples. That's the way
it was for him—he bumped into something
he'd written, the handwriting his. What happened
to the man who wrote that? The man who once believed
he might become a saint? Dreams can own a man
and chain him like a dog. He confesses to loving
winter trees when their leafless limbs sadden
the barren earth with their unbearable lack
of irony. Imagine standing naked night after
night, your arms stretched out, daring the wind
to take you down, your roots clawing and clamping
down on the frozen soil. What is a storm in the face
of a stubborn tree? *The morning lights the limbs. The earth
is new again.* Another fragment among unfinished
writings. The man who wrote those words is gone,
dead and glad too, though there are days he mourns
him. He is done with heaven. He prefers the earth,
the dirt, the words he hears on the lips of other men.
Today the sky is cloudless blue, serene in the aftermath
of a storm. He spent the day in stillness, a boy
memorizing the subtle shadows of the sky. Tired
he slept. He dreamed a tree, leafless, standing alone
in a windless night.

        He dreamed a lonely road—
the starry night pelting him with a rain of letters
struggling to turn themselves into words.

The News of the Day

Bodies get dumped in empty lots and roadsides, heaped together
in cases of massacre or laid out alone if that's how the victim
died. Police recover corpses stuffed in cars, tumbled into clandestine
tombs, laid out like scrabble pieces to form letters.

He—the man—is reading the newspaper
on the internet: a photographer is taking black
ink and writing *Boycott hate* on people's arms.
The photographer dresses his subjects in white—
he is creating an army of tattooed angels.

Today, four journalists were kidnapped in Durango.
This will be the man's morning prayer, their names
on his lips *Jaime. Hector. Oscar. Alejandro.*

The man stares into the sweet face of the photographer
who, like his subjects, dresses himself in white.
He too looks like an angel. The man is reading
what the photographer has to say about his work.
The artist is articulate. He is intelligent. He is handsome.
He is an innocent. He has not spent much time hiking
the bloody and unforgiving terrain of the Americas.
The artist believes the world can be touched
by a dream. By a photograph.

In Juárez, two headless bodies lie bleeding
on the street. They have been posed there by
performance artists. The bystanders pick up the notes
pinned to their bodies. They stand on the sidewalk—
and read the lines with terror. They all have their assigned
roles. There is a part for everyone to play. This is the new
democracy. This is the only theater that is left.

This is what the man
is thinking: To spend your days looking at the faces
of young men who don't yet wear the cruelty
of the world on their scarless skins. To spend
your days like that. Journalists find their bodies
on the streets of Juárez or Baghdad or Qandahar.
This is how the nations train them to be men.

*With decapitations becoming almost cliché, now arms and legs
get severed too. One victim in Cuidad Juárez was found crucified
on a chain link fence with a pig's head attached to his torso.
Another reportedly had his face stitched to a soccer ball.*

*God, send an angel over the waters
of chaos and make it new again.* A prayer the man once uttered
in a moment of belief.
Jaime, Hector, Oscar, Alejandro.

＊

A day after soldiers and investigators uncovered the graves,
the yard stood abandoned. Attention turned to the bodies
of four young men dumped last week in a busy intersection
in Monterrey and to gun battles in Nuevo Laredo.

＊

A student writes to him and asks: you know about anger.
You conjure that so well. Is there any happiness? Or joy?

How can he find his innocence again?
How can he conjure joy in such a world as this?

MEDITATION

Tonight he has lost his faith. Now
he understands that none of this
will ever end. He does not want
to be consoled. He does not want to avert
his eyes. All he knows is blood. All he knows
is fire. Guns. Thunder. He searches
the sky for—but he does, he does want
to avert his eyes. For once in his goddamned
life, he would like to live without the news
of the day. For once. For once
in his goddamned life, he would like
to bathe in the quiet of his own sweet
words and place a paradise
of sentences on a perfect page.

You

Once you thought you knew where you were going.

ROADS

1.

Reading Robert Frost ruined roads for you.

Those two roads converging scared and screwed you up.

It was as if you were being forced to make a decision about your life *before you had a life*.

You'd think and think about the roads.

One day you decided to decide.

You bought a pack of cigarettes.

And fell in love with smoking.

That was the road you took.

Not a good decision.

But smoking gave you a life.

And that has made all the difference.

2.

You are always photographing roads.

You're never happy with the outcome.

Happiness isn't everything. Not that you'd know.

You keep thinking you'll take a perfect picture—someday—of a road.

Lonely and beautiful.

You love only lonely roads.

You have no patience with traffic and crowded freeways.

Being a lover of roads has never turned you into a good driver.

You never know where you're going.

All you want is a camera and an empty road that disappears into the horizon as if it were a part of nature.

The open road is larger and more generous than anything Jack Kerouac ever imagined.

Kerouac never knew where he was going either.

If you would have met Kerouac, you would probably have fallen in love with him.

3.

You can't bear Kerouac.

You suspect he was in love with all the tricks his penis could do.

That's why he always had to hit the road.

He always got himself into penis trouble.

He was a pre-feminist unreconstructed man's man.

That doesn't mean he wasn't beautiful.

See, you would have fallen in love with him.

You have this thing with hands—the way they move and betray all the secrets you keep.

Hands don't have it in them to lie.

4.

You wonder if anyone has taken a really close look at the hands on the figures of a Velázquez painting?

Those hands are forever longing, forever reaching, forever hungry.

They belong to the hands of saints.

They look like the hands of Jews in concentration camps, fleshless and pale.

You wish those hands could touch you.

They would be like a road.

They would take you to a country you've never seen.

To a place where the shadows touch the sun.

Avenida Juárez. May 7, 2010. 12:37 a.m.

Young soldiers, rifles slung over their shoulders, pace the dead and empty street.

Seven people laze out of the Kentucky Club, searching their pockets, looking for change to pay the toll. Charon does not take money from the living—but the turnstile is hungry for coins. Sober in their drunkenness, these ragged pilgrims place their quarters in the slots and begin their journey home. They carry the weight of the evening, carry the weight of this sad and singular thought: Juárez is no longer alive. Juárez is no longer alive.

The immigration agent checks the passport of a young woman: *What were you doing in Juárez? Do you have a death wish?* When he asks the next man in line if he has anything to declare, the man laughs: *I would like to declare my sadness. I would like to declare that all my dreams are dead.*

A man—alone—is making his way over the bridge. No hurry in his steps. He remembers another time, the streets full and teeming with commerce and expectation. He stares out into the lights of El Paso, his back to Juárez. He listens to the echoes of the empty streets. The laughter and dancing are gone. Nostalgia is his only consolation.

A handsome man, well-dressed, in his early thirties, rushes across the bridge. In twenty minutes he will be dancing in the nightclubs of El Paso. If the killings never stop, then neither does the dancing.

Juárez: The Last Ode
Spring

1.

When the killing started, they cut off their hands.

There were stories in the newspapers.

The water in the river began to disappear.

No one wrote about the water.

The people of Juárez began to leave.

There were more stories in the newspapers.

They cut off their hands. They cut off their legs.

The river disappeared.

*

Those who stayed behind were getting killed.

*

The trees have decided to die.

*

There is no more touching.

*

The reporters who wrote the stories in the newspapers began to disappear.

*

Sometimes they cut off their heads.

*

The trees are abandoning all their leaves.

*

Juárez is a city of empty houses.

*

The sparrows are falling from the sky.

*

The trees are dying.

*

The newspapers are afraid to talk about the empty houses.

It will never rain again.

The blue in the sky is disappearing.

The green leaves are in exile.

Those who left stopped dreaming of a return.

The last sparrow has fallen from the sky.

There are no reporters left to tell the stories.

Some are lost in the desert looking for the women who were buried there.

There are no hands left to hold through the long night.

2.

They have torn down all the buildings. Not even the façade of the Cathedral was left standing.

*

The bridge survives. No one remembers where it went or why it was built.

*

Juárez is only a memory. Already we are forgetting how the world used to be.

*

The world lives on. In silence.

3.

Sparrows' eggs are scattered all over El Paso.

*

The clouds are organizing themselves.

*

Soon the rains will return.

*

The sparrows' eggs are hatching.

*

The trees have decided to live.

*

It is beginning to rain.

Water is flowing through the river.

The sparrows have hatched.

The trees are forcing themselves to grow new leaves.

The rain has become a downpour.

The water in the river is raging.

The sparrows are learning to fly.

The green leaves of the trees that decided to live are reaching out to catch the rain.

When the rain stops, there is nothing but the sound of the raging waters of the river.

The sky is full of sparrows singing.

Juárez has reappeared in El Paso.

The streets are flowing with people.

Everyone is listening to the songs of the sparrows.

The people have discovered their hands again.

The dead have come back to tell their stories.

The reporters are writing down every word.

The people are clapping.

Everyone is crying.

The people are embracing.

Everyone is speaking Spanish.

People are crossing over the bridge.

The voices of the women who were buried in the desert are leading the people back home.

The night is disappearing into a perfect sky.

On Caring and Not Caring: You and I and We

There are emotional empaths
Strewn all over the world—a diaspora of suffering souls,
Absorbing the pain of others. You can care too much. Imagine
Running into perfect strangers and sensing their afflictions.
Imagine taking on their hurts. *I feel your pain* is not simply
A throw-away line uttered for a laugh by a late night
Comedian. *I feel your pain*. Imagine holding on to that phrase. Not
Just on your tongue but in the softest part of your flesh,
The part that's most likely to bruise, the part that's tender
To the touch. Touch. Bruise. That's a part of the pain thing.
You have to let yourself be touched. No, not by the guy
With the straight teeth who's wearing a shirt he takes
To the cleaners. Not by him. But by the guy standing
Next to you at the 7-11 who's about to break down
In tears and smells like he hasn't bathed in a month. He needs
A drink. He needs a bath. He needs water. He needs more
Than you can ever give him. You know, that guy. You have
Already made up a story about him and his pedestrian
Afflictions. About how you can't change the course
Of his life. About how he can't change the course of yours.
He's not a man. He's a cliché. Touch. Caring. Jesus suffered
From this psychological condition. An emotional empath
If there ever was one. I would have loved to be his therapist.
I would have fallen in love with his voice. I would have let him
Touch me. I would have tried to stop him from dying
On a cross and intervened in salvation history. Maybe
Interventions aren't always such a good idea. Therapists
Falling in love with their patients. I have a theory about this.
It's not Freudian. Only therapists who are doing their job
Fall in love with their patients. Maybe the right word
Isn't love. The right word is compassion. We're back to

Empathy. Counter transference. That's another term
For caring too much. Caring. It isn't safe to care. It never
Was. Any time you encounter another's pain, anything
can happen. It isn't pretty. Things can get violent.
The possibility of being lost, being swallowed whole
Is there, is real, is calling your name. A new vocation.
And you want to be swallowed—whole—you do, finally
Giving yourself up. God, giving yourself up. But
There's that terrifying possibility that you may never
Return to the serene world you cherish. What
About all that money you saved? There's always
Cash involved. Just as there's always a choice. Money
In the bank or the chance to care. You hate this math.
To touch another's pain—like touching the white
Of the purest cloud of summer just as its about to let loose
The rain. Most people run for cover. Some brave bastards
Dive into the storm. People die every day. In storms.
The chaos of another's pain can do a better job of drowning
You than any pedestrian flood Nature can throw at you.
Me. You. I. We. Us. Things can get really crowded
And complicated in your head. You can care too much. About
Things and people who aren't worth caring about.
Think of the woman who stays despite the bruises. What
Does her heart look like when she stares into the eyes
Of her man? The man who can only say love
With a closed fist? Love can be as twisted and grotesque
As any Wes Craven horror flick. You used to care
About the yard. Your version of money
In the bank. All that time wasted on caring about
A garden. It's true, you're still in love with desert
Plants. Plants are easier to love than people. You
Felt their pain. You mourned for the ones
That didn't make it. Sometimes you cried. That's the sorry
Truth. You blamed yourself. You'll never learn.

You could run
Out to the store *right now* and buy a pack of Marlboros. But
What's the use? The thrill is gone. That long affair
With cigarettes. What a waste. You used to care about
Friends you don't even know anymore. How many people
Can you love anyway? Love may be infinite but the human heart
Has its limits. That's why they've built a wall between us
And Mexico. Think about the guy at the 7-11. How many
People *can* you love? How many weddings can you attend
Without throwing your hands up in despair? Ever wonder
Why people drink too much at weddings? Emotional empaths
All over the place. *Poor bastards.* Imagine suffering
From all that love. And then there's that don't-give-a-shit
Attitude that will take you straight to hell. The not caring.
You know about this one. Maybe that's the real problem.
Some people care more about their guns than the people
Who get shot by them. They care too much about
The meanest part of the Bill of Rights. What is that
About? Why is everyone always preparing for war?
What does an automatic assault rifle on the streets
Of Atlanta have to do with freedom? Somehow, you don't
Believe gun lovers qualify as emotional empaths. To hell
With them. You mean it. You don't care about them. See?
Where is all your caring? All your compassion? In the large
Cracks and crevices between the caring and not caring—
That's where you live. That's your permanent address.

SNOW

You must not become a mere peddler of words. The thing to learn is to
know what people are thinking about, not what they say.
—Kate Swift

It does not matter that Kate Swift only existed as a character in a town called Winesburg, Ohio. Readers have their prerogatives. And in this case, the author is dead. It's Kate who lives. You resurrect her every time you pick up Anderson's book. Resurrect is a word you fell in love with while studying Catholic theology, a word you cannot exile from the dictionary you keep on a shelf in your brain.

Kate had been a teacher. She was subject to mood swings, always a battle raging within. The children were scared of her. The children loved her. Behind a cold exterior the most extraordinary things transpired in her mind. You are picturing yourself as one of her students. You are watching your hands move through the air, trying to make yourself see what she alone can see.

She liked to lie down on her bed and read though you suspect reading a book was just an excuse for her to light up another cigarette. You are watching the cigarette touch her lips. She is smoking Marlboro Lights.

She took a walk one night in the middle of a snowstorm. Tonight there is snow falling in Atlanta and Dallas. The nation's capital is under a foot of snow. It is snowing everywhere in the American South. It is below freezing in Iowa City. You lived there once. Only for a year. It felt like a lifetime. You read a lot. You smoked your heart out. Smoking helped you survive the lonely cold. You are watching the cigarette touch your lips. You are smoking Marlboro

Lights. You have never been so cold. You are in love with the frozen river and feeling the smoke in your lungs as the snow falls.

You are wondering what it would be like to be Kate Swift, wondering what it would be like to be a woman, what it would be like to take George Willard and kiss that boy like he had never been kissed before.

Kate is walking through a snowstorm. The landscape of winter disappears. The theater of the mind is all that's left and all that matters.

What does George know, at eighteen? He yearns—and does not even know enough to know what he is yearning for. Kate is kissing him. Kissing and kissing and kissing him. He could live in that storm forever.

Kate is looking into George's eyes *he does not understand my kisses. He does not understand.*

You are watching George Willard walking through a storm. George, he is a man now. He likes the feel of the cold. He likes to watch the snow fall. He is muttering, he is muttering *I have missed something. I have missed something.* But it is too late. He knows he will never kiss Kate again.

READING NOVELS

Keep telling yourself this: *my life is as lovely as the morning dew.*
There's a thought. Or tell yourself this: *Shit! I have wasted*
Most of my life hating myself. Thoughts that cross the mind
Have a logic all their own. Let's not bring logic into this.
You don't know anything about physics or math. You just had
A conversation with your younger sister. Logic had nothing
To do with your conversation. You could talk to her forever.
She's better than a character in a novel. Together, you can
Laugh. Hell, sometimes you cry. Together. You're glad
You know words. You're glad they live inside you. So
You can talk to your sister—the one that's better than
Any novel. You know, you can't talk without words. Can you?
But can you think without them? Or are thoughts outside
The kingdom of language? Is thinking without language
Like having sex without sexual organs? You remember
Studying this very question when you were in a philosophy
Class in college. You were an awful philosophy student. You
Needed to be good at logic. You don't remember the answer
To the question about the relationship between thought
And language. They let you smoke in class back then.
Maybe you were lost in smoke. Maybe you were trying to put
The way smoke felt in your lungs into language. Maybe you were
Trying to write a short story that you hoped would grow up
To be a novel. Maybe you were just bored, bored, bored
And daydreaming (in language?)—maybe that's why you don't
Remember the answer. On some days, you don't remember
Anything. You have to make yourself think hard, breathe deep,
Stay perfectly still. Sometimes you have to think a long time
Before you remember the names of the main characters
Of the novel you're reading. You picture them, the characters.
You think of the way they inflect words, the way they turn

Away when they don't want to hear the voice
Of the person who is hurting them—or telling them
The truth. You always feel sorry for them and talk to them
As if they existed. *But they do exist. They do. You swear they do*!
You tell them things *Don't do it don't do it* but they always do it.
The wrong thing. *Shit*! They mean well. They're smart.
They know things. Things that matter. Things about
The darkness and the light. They want to be better.
They're tired of living their days, making the same mistakes.
They're tired of hating themselves. They're tired of waking up
To lives they don't want anymore. They need. They reach.
They ache. When they're alone, they're articulate and intelligent.
But something happens when they're in a room with
Other people. There is always something that prevents them
From attaining happiness. Hell, it's too painful to watch
These people screwing up their lives. *And you can't even turn away*
Because you're reading! They're beautiful, the characters
In all the novels you love. Keep telling yourself this: *My life*
Is as beautiful as the morning dew. Then tell yourself this: *Shit*!
I have wasted my life hating myself. Just finish reading your novel.

With the Flu: Lying In Bed For Days

You are in a house with many rooms with your ex-wife. You are touring the rooms. You both sit in front of a fireplace where the stone is cold and there is no fire. You know the house will not make her happy. You know the house will not make you happy either. But you know you are going to buy the house.

You are in high school. You are a tennis player. You are returning a serve and then realize you are naked and have a hard on. Everyone is watching. There is nowhere to hide.

The morning sun streaming through the window feels like a sliver of glass embedded in your brain.

You want to repent of all your stupidities. You have said this to yourself before. You start listing your stupidities. You stop yourself. You have made this list before.

You are walking through the desert. The wind is cold and you have no coat. You forgot your shoes when you left the house. Your feet are bleeding, but the cold helps you not to feel.

You are driving your truck and the steering wheel disappears. You are trying to take your foot off the gas pedal, but your foot will not move.

You keep sleeping. You keep waking. Sleeping and waking and dreaming. Sleeping and waking and dreaming. You cannot break the endless cycle. Finally you force yourself to rise from your bed. You stumble toward the kitchen in search of a glass of water. When you feel the water on your tongue, you know that no liquid exists that can quench your thirst. You feel your whole body shaking. You have never been this cold. Everything is dark. You manage to stumble back to bed. And you sleep.

You are disappearing into the desert. You will become one with all the bodies of the women who were lost there. Together you and they will become a we. And we will all rise from the dead and haunt the world until the killings stop. You smile at the thought and when you wake, you are happy. You have never been this hungry. You make potato soup. You sit and eat and think of the hundreds of different varieties of potatoes that the Incas grew in their ancient kingdom. The Incas knew no hunger. You take a shower. The hot water against your skin makes you feel young though you know you will never be young again.

You think it would be okay to die. You think, no, no, there is still so much to say. And then you think of a damaged man you met, a man who did some time, who clothed his chest in tattoos, who reeked of cigarettes and crack, who smiled like a boy, who asked you to buy him a burger, who swore to you he was going into rehab. You think of him, his sad eyes, and know that he has never been loved and you understand that the darkest part of your heart leaps toward him and you want *you want* to love him. You lie in bed in horror and see his eyes staring into yours. You breathe and breathe and breathe. You send him away with a poem:

> There is nothing I can do about your life.
> I'm not your father, lover, not your wife.

There is no distinguishing the truth, a dream, what happens in the mind when the body is on fire, and Carlos, is he here? *He is here.* He is pacing the rooms looking for something he has lost. He is pacing and pacing and asking himself *is it here? Is it here?* He wakes you and asks you questions you can't answer. You tell him to leave you alone, tell him that you are sick and need to sleep. You hear him leave the room. You hear him continue his pacing. You want to tell him that he will not find what he is looking for. What he has lost is not here. You fall asleep again. Or maybe you fell asleep while you were asleep. A dream within a dream. A life within a life. When you wake, Carlos is gone. Or maybe he was never there. You take a shower and you know that you are awake. The water is hot on your skin and you feel clean. Your stomach is empty. But you are too hungry to eat so you find a book and begin to read. When you wake again, the book is in your hands. The book is real.

There is a hotel room but where is the bed? You walk down the halls and all the doors are open and people are sleeping. Why do they have beds? You don't remember how to get back into your room, can't find it, don't and can't remember which floor. You get into an elevator and there is a party going on. Young men are drinking and snorting cocaine. You know some of the young men but cannot remember their names. You are not in a hotel anymore. You are in the patio of a bar and the night is warm and the lights are dim so that no one can see the truth. The young men sit around, drunk and high, and then you start remembering their names: Tony and Carlos and Marcus and Ben and they are all singing in perfect harmony. You are sitting alone, listening. When you wake, you can still hear the singing of young men and the soft notes of a piano. But you are not really awake because you are in a house and an old woman is sitting in a hospital bed in the middle of the living room. You know the woman. She is your ex-mother-in-law. She disapproves of you. You cannot leave the room because the doors have disappeared. You have to live in the judgment of her stare. You tell yourself to wake. You tell yourself to wake.

You take a hot shower, change the rancid sheets—and feel yourself trembling. And then Carlos is sitting on your bed, telling you about all the things in his life that have hurt him and you tell him you're sorry about his pain. You tell him you will take away his pain and put it next to yours and his pain and your pain will live together inside you. And then Daniel is sitting on your bed and he tells you about the day his mother died and he is crying and you tell him you will take his pain and put it next to yours. Then Ginny is sitting on your bed and she tells you of all the hurt, all the hurt. And then you tell her you will take away her pain and that it will live next to yours inside of you. She looks at you and tells you that the pain is hers, that you cannot have it. And Michael tells you that it is raining and that the rain will never stop. He takes your hand and tells you that you will not always be sick. And you tell him you will be well when it stops raining. And now Karen is sitting on your bed and you see all the compassion of the world in her eyes and she tells you that when you wake, there will be another storm, but you will be alive again. You are no longer stupid enough to tell her that you will take her pain—because the pain is hers.

Again you wake. Again you are drenched in sweat. You peel off your clothes and you are taking another shower. You are grateful for the kindness of a soft towel. You are grateful for clean underwear and clean t-shirts and you cannot stop from shaking but you feel safe because your bed is clean and you are clean. And then Carlos is sitting on your bed again and you tell him you have to give him back his pain. And he says *I have missed it*. And he smiles. You are happy and light because you understand that the only pain you have to carry is your own. You think it all must be a dream, but in the dream you fall asleep and do not dream again.

You wake to the sounds of a storm. The wind is fierce and the snow, angry and relentless. The days go by and you don't know what is wrong, but then one night, you fall asleep again. There is nothing but sleeping and waking and sleeping and waking and when you wake once more, the sun is shining. You step out into the day and breathe in the desert air. You have been on a journey. But you're back now. You drink a cup of coffee. Twenty-eight people have been killed in Juárez since the day you got the flu. And this thought enters your head: you will have to learn to live with your own insanity. You will have to learn to live among the dead.

JACOB'S LADDER
In memory of Denise Levertov

There are no angels on this ladder. Jacob,
always on a journey, addicted to his pilgrimage. Eyes
searching for God, always traveling through
the desert. If a holy man cannot find his God, he prefers
the solitude and cruelty of the burning sands. A holy man
has no interest in comfort. A holy man has no
interest in the talk of idle men. Offer him a piece
of bread but do not offer him coins. Offer him
water but do not offer him wine. Do not
offer him words.

       Jacob. He used a stone for a pillow
and dreamed. You have given up on holiness but you have *not yet*
given up on ladders. Sometimes you picture a young man
sitting on a ladder, reading a book, the earth below him.
Maybe he is reading the Bible. But you doubt it. This is
your brain drawing the picture. You think it more certain
he is reading a book of poems or a strange story
by J.G. Ballard. You never know whether that young man
on that ladder is you. You try not to spend your time
on questions of identity. Those questions can never
be solved. In any case you are no longer young—though
a young man still clings to the stubborn corners
of your body. The young man inside you
has an inoperable tumor and likes to laugh. He likes
to cry. He likes to read. He likes to climb on ladders.
He likes to ascend and then descend, traveling in between
the heavens and the earth. Maybe the young man
sitting on the ladder is an angel. So the young
man can*not* possibly be you.
       He must be Jacob as a young man.

You are staring at
one of Manuel Álvarez Bravo's photographs. Diego
Rivera is standing on a ladder. He is painting
a mural. For Rivera, a ladder is a tool. You do not believe
Rivera gave ladders much thought. He was not
the kind of man that appreciated the things
he stepped on. In another photograph, an old man
named Francisco is sitting on a ladder. Francisco
is a peasant. For him, a ladder is a place of rest.
In another, a ladder is leaning against the wall.
According to the title, the ladder is there *para
subir el cielo*. Richie Valens is singing that phrase
over and over in your head. The only thing you need
to reach the sky is a ladder. A good ladder
is made of wood. It is a resurrected tree. You like
to imagine that leaves can sprout from every step
of that good ladder. You see leaves everywhere.
Sometimes the sky is full of them. Leaves falling
to earth, floating, becoming birds, becoming
pages full of words, descending—but never
ascending. The Rabbi claims that the angels' descent
and ascent are dependent on his actions. If
he forgives, the angels will ascend. If he sins,
the angels will descend and live in exile on
the bitter ground. The Rabbi is arrogant. What
depends on what *you* do? You want words to ascend.
You want to believe this. You are staring at the ladder.
Can you ask the young man living inside you to
help you climb? Can you order him *Climb! Climb! Climb!*

I

Then one fine morning—

PRAYER

Winter is leafless and cold. I am reaching
towards summer

It was a long time ago

      a boy, small, who walked in sadness
through cotton fields, who sat in the shade
to escape the heat of another punitive
summer. Who imagined he lived alone
in a jungle as he stared up at the sky
through the thicket of the dark green leaves. Who
would study the clouds and pray for rain—though
he did not know he was praying. I think now
the boy knew nothing of prayer. He could not
fathom a god who cared enough, who had
time enough to listen to a common boy
who spoke a common language.

                                    Please
the first word that always seemed to arrive on his lips
though he had few words to pick from in his
limited and insignificant vocabulary. *Please* he knew
it to be a kind of begging in his prideless chest. Was
it rain? Is that what he wanted? New shoes? A room
full of books? There was a world cluttered with cities—
and he tried to imagine those cities, crowded
with cars and men and women who wore expensive
clothes and read magazines and newspapers
as they sat and drank their coffee, men and women
who read of the kindness and cruelties of
the swelling and swallowing streets, and scanned

the pages looking for better jobs. Work is a word
he knew. It was what he was born for. Work
his future, his fate, his destiny.

Is it too late to go back? To tell the boy
that his wounded heart is holding a sea
of tears—to tell him he must learn to swim
in other waters. To tell him to hurl the hurt
out into the open sky. To hold him and to whisper
in his tender ear that the country of exile
is no playground for a boy who yearns
to laugh. To take his hand and lead him
to the place where the river begins, brimming
with the waters of spring. Is it too late?
For me? To save the boy?

For Carlos

I.

Tuesday, and again I wake to thoughts of you. Love
is a weight we carry. Today, this prayer
on my lips: *Let me bear this, let me bear it, let me walk
the ground with grace.* Annie Lennox in the air, the lonely
lilt of her voice, each note a tear *You turn to face the day
and love don't show up in...* A cup of coffee, a book,
my fingers on a charcoal sketch—and these few
words will save me for today. *Steady steady* a smile
for the mirror—then listen to a song, then another.
Make the lost boy be the man he wants to be. *Steady
Steady* and when I see—*Enough! Get dressed and ready.
Walk out the door. Maybe, baby, maybe my love will be gone*

*and I will not ache to take your hands in mine
and stare into your palms and memorize each line.*

II.

You and me, cleaning my apartment. Many nights have passed
since first I brought you here—and we did coke. You were
the teacher, I the bewildered student so eager and hungry
to learn. You were so at ease—showing me paintings
of an artist you admired, your hands animated, the curiosity
in your voice filling the autumn night. I did not know then
I would love. I did not know, *not then*, that in a future time

you would be a storm. You would be the sound of falling rain.
And here we are: men with different spellings of the same last name

cleaning, cleaning. I listen to the mop on the surface of the floor.
I hear the swish of water and the closing of a door.

You, in the next room, mopping, wiping, working,
I picture the intent look in your eyes and want to be the echo
of the song that you are softly whistling. I let the sunlight
bathe my face. I'll take this day and what it has to give. Another
move for me, another place to hang my hat. And you? How
many houses in a lifetime? How many treasures lost
in all those moves? *But their loss is no disaster. Practice losing
farther, losing faster*

                                                                    You and me.
In different rooms. Once I loved this place and made it mine.
I was just a passing tenant. That love is spent. It's time—

III.

One summer, but *not* summer, not in Tanzania.
And I was young and sweeter than a mango (though
I was blind to sweetness), I saw a perfect boy
steal a perfect leaf from a banana tree. He held it tight
above his head. The rain poured down and he defied
the storm with nothing but that leaf. He waved
at me and I waved back. I have kept and loved
that scene, have stored it in my memory all
these thirty years. I love the taste of coffee, hot
and black and bitter as it wakes me from my slumber.
I love the morning sun as it slices through the windows
in my house. My dog is sitting on my lap—his clear
and curious eyes look up at me with a wonder
and an innocence I've long since lost. I love
a summer sky, the clouds that throw me back
to shirtless boyhood days. I love the echoes
of a singer in my head. I love the silence as I walk
a desert trail. I love the smoothness and the coldness

of a rock—the way I warm it as I rub it in my patient
patient palms. I love the smell of lumber as I
cut it with a saw. I love the stretching of the canvas
the colors on the brush as I force the paint
and bend it to my will. My mind's alert and clear
when I sit in search of words—

        and I am more alive than any god.

       But always there are shadows lurking in my
crooked heart. In my bent and crooked heart.

The boy in Tanzania. The dog, the coffee and the light.

I love. I love you more than that.

IV.

    They were being loved?
    Amabantur
    I shall be loved?
    Amabor
    You will have been loved?
    Amatus eris.

Love is a language I have never—
       nothing like the English on my tongue or the Spanish

in my dreams.

I lie on the fallow fields of all my paragraphs and poems.

    In a mother's arms, I learned the verb to love. It was she
who knew that verb, she who practiced loving day by day, week by
week until the weeks became the years became her life. She knew
the austere cruelty of that word and all its sufferings and silences
and all its awful pain. To love—she owned that verb. I'm not
enough my mother—too much my father's son.

The sun streaming through my window is a river of light. I want to drink it down. Some days I want to live without the darkness.

To hold you close and breathe. Take in the smell of your skin as if it were the last cigarette on earth. To feel your touch, to feel your fingers on my back.

To think that once my love for you was fire
And now my heart has leapt beyond desire.

V.

Now, when the day is almost done, and the tired, ancient sun takes its final step before it sinks and dies, tell me. Tell me again what we said, the words we spoke, how we wasted hours almost drowning in an ocean of meth and misunderstanding—and never touched. How we hurt and wept, how one fine day we woke young and saw this same sad sun, new and rising with a fire that raged like your eyes when first I saw and loved you.

I see your face on every wall, in every corner of the room. I write a word, stop, then sputter—I stutter and then start. I want to speak your name. *Now*! You're gone. Soon your name will be a fragment in my slow and idiot heart.

VI.

November Sunday morning—my house an empty church. No saints, no priests, and no believers. My heart beats out a quiet, crooked prayer, if prayer's what it is. I roam the rooms, waking, wandering through days and weeks and months so badly spent. Why look for what is lost and can't be found? *I stepped here and here and here. I did this and I did that. I said what? To whom? I said what to him? To you?* I don't recall the stupid

angry words but still recall the madness in their faces
with something beatific in their eyes. There are names
of men I did not know or love graffitied on the bare
and barren walls. Confetti in the night—garbage
in the morning. *I said this and you said—*

       Carlos, no survivors in the war called *blame.*
In the quiet, quiet of this room—in the seductive flame

       that burned beneath a meth pipe, your face
in the shadows of the dawn—ahh, such are
the aesthetics of addiction. Soldiers, angels, shit! We fight
ourselves in separate corners. All we were was broken.
To think I live my hours straightening out my days
with verbs and nouns and adjectives.

I can't write my nights out of this one.

       I'll never get it—never find
the source of why I loved you. *The heart goes where
it goes.* Isn't that what you said as we sat one day
in a park? My heart shot straight toward you. And
yours in an opposite direction. My books are packed.
I'm giving some away. Some I'll never part with. I'm not
brave enough to live my life with nothing—so I'm boxing
what I can. Some things don't fit in books
      and can't be read away.

       What I'm living now is only half a life.
Losing you was more than half the fight.

       Mourning your voice was the worst. Now
that you're finally gone, I'm grieving something else.
The meth, the booze, apocalyptic nights, nothing
new, nothing out of the ordinary, dime store addict,
common as a pigeon, common as a rat in a sewer, nothing
you haven't lived yourself. There's nothing I can teach

you. Hell, I was only an apprentice. I never met a man
with your skill and expertise. The way you held
the pipe and—ahh, such are the aesthetics
of addiction. I'm not the first to take this road and sadly
not the last. Still a love's a love. All the other ones
were only stand-ins. All those nights spent chasing
the dream of a dragon that always managed to escape—
and all the while my stoned heart whispering your name.
The past is as near as the next hit you take. *Good times, good
times*. That's your voice echoing through
this empty temple of a house. No one could whistle
in the dark better than you. I may be an idiot, easily played
like a passive guitar yearning to be touched—look, I'm not
nostalgic. I'm living in today. I'm living in the stark
beauty of a desert dawn. Have you heard? There's a sun.
It hurts my eyes to look into the light. It's not so bad. Hurt
is nothing new. I could show you every scar, who
put it there and when. And even where. I could show
you every wound. I'm learning the lessons of the skin—
and moving on. Another life. Live them and leave them.
I won't be giving you a forwarding address. But
it won't matter. You never could find where I lived.
I'm taking stock of everything I've lost: that gray coat
I loved, money, that expensive pair of glasses, money,
an iPod, money, an iPad, two iPhones (was it three?),
sleep, the me I used to know. Relax! Relax! You never
took a thing I didn't let you take. Except that photograph
of you—your back to me. That's all you had to give.
That's what I'll take. One day without my alcohol and
meth becomes a week, becomes a month, becomes a year.

I have a life you said with the conviction of a drowning man.

One day, one week, one month and soon enough a year.
Your face will fade, your voice will disappear.

VII.

There is the missing you. Today, that's all. Nothing
more. I live in the music of a heart struggling to word out
a song. And *shit*! me born with this regrettable voice.
Last night, a dream: I was on the balcony. I looked down
at the street and watched you disappear into a thunderous
rain. Me, knowing there would be no return—but
looking out, all the same. Only the sound of pounding
rain. The pounding, pounding rain.
I could say I shouted out your name—
                    but that's a lie.

I can't say precisely when I began to notice. Precision?
Not my forte. I'm not a mathematician. But
it was there, that cruel and awful yearning, clawing at
an already confused and complicated heart. Why
was it there, that yearning? Why did it choose to visit
me again? When does it stop? When does it stop?
If I were only a boy again, I could dismiss it all
with ease. The doors to original innocence are
locked. The days are done when I can just pretend.

I'd like to think we had a season we called ours.
Just a thought. Just a pretty, pretty thought. I'll miss
your gestures, certainly, I'll miss the laughter
in your eyes. I'll miss the way you lost and interrupted
your own stories as you spoke. I'll miss the way you lit
a cigarette. I could say: *I'll miss your touch*. But then—
that touch—it was a fiction conjured by a churning,
yearning heart. Proof I
            can miss the thing I never had.

                    I could say I was sorry.
Another lie. This is not what I wanted. *This is not what
I meant at all*. The missing you. The sadness. I suppose

I could live in regret—which is to say I often wish I was another man. But the part of me that loved you? That? That I can't regret.

Martin Luther King Day 2010

Monday in January driving up Mesa Street nice day sunny a break between cold fronts a young man maybe seventeen sixteen twenty nice-looking holding up a sign *Need Help: family kidnapped in Juárez* don't look don't pretend not to see him! try to see him! His face sad uncomfortable uneasy not used to begging on the streets of El Paso or any street on this poor and broken city that's no more poor or broken than any other American city except we're painfully obvious unable to hide we throw our brokenness up in the air in hopes it will fall back to earth as light as confetti in a fucking parade let's not get all Charles Dickens here the kid's not Pip he's real and actual and interactive but definitely not like the beggars who sit on the Santa Fe Bridge who long ago banished the word *dignity* from their vocabularies who barely have enough water to drink water for a bath a dream and when they thrust out their hands I don't I don't want touch don't want touch I am as dirty dirtier keep pretending I'm clean let's not get too superior mistake well-bathed with clean we're all covered in our own shit some of us appear almost beautiful have good dentists or practice good hygiene or have good genes which is not the same thing as virtue I keep looking into his face *family kidnapped* I know confusion been teaching young men his age for twenty years too long not to know that look not like the veterans who sit around my street sitting around like crows banished from the flock veterans of a war that refuses to end which is life which is life right and yeah there's another fucking war right here on the border but these guys haven't gotten over the one they fought who could get over bombs exploding in your dreams veterans who drink eighteen percent wine who've lost themselves mentally ill not strong morally bankrupt hurt as hell can't afford anymore to be moral an expensive proposition someone hurt them hurt now they don't give a damn shit in the alley don't give a howling coyote who sees their brokenness that word again and it's over for them though they will go on living if that's what it is and who gets to decide what living is me you the Catholic Church and is it over for Juárez and what would I do if I lived there move here like they'd let me in oh yeah sure come on over and *this guy this clean-cut kid with the sign this kid what am I we supposed to make of him* all of this he's not a pro knows what a bath is knows what shame is lost doesn't want to be lost dark eyes looks American Americans have a look even Americans who are Mexican and live on the border Chicano Latino keeps blinking his eyes like he's going to cry like he's been crying all morning like he'll go home if he has a home *he must have* I want him to he's clean bathed go home break down cry forever *Please Help: family kidnapped in Juárez* the end of history, the end of the world, the end of civilization maybe he's a fraud maybe he's a good liar *liar*! he's just exploiting the headlines someone got beheaded the other day how medieval is that *London Bridge is falling down falling* the pregnant girl who worked at Jimmy's got killed boyfriend into drugs what was the latest number two hundred three hundred one thousand this is the way we teach our children how to count and how many people have moved into El Paso and how many restaurants and businesses and now El Paso is thriving while Juárez dies can a city die? I never thought a city could actually die but this kid he's just exploiting the whole bloody is this what Wallace Stevens meant *We live in an old chaos of the sun* yes *he is* taking advantage of the situation he is we can get angry at a boy holding a sign instead of feeling a little compassion maybe we'll fall for the whole sham hand him a few bucks he'll have a drink make the world right and the world *will be right* in one of these nice little bar and grills next to the university where all the cars stop for red lights where everything is all order nobody knows anything about anybody who is that boy with the sign is his family kidnapped how many mother father sister baby brother who why what is the real story the woman next to me talking on her cell as her son stares out the window dreaming of and I drive away and why didn't I stop and ask what the real story was *why didn't I ask* because I fucking don't want to know write

something beautiful I have a dream and you have a dream and we
all have another beautiful lie

that will help us forget.

HERE IT IS ONCE AGAIN

Here it is once again this one note
from a string of longing
—W.S. Merwin

Each morning, a knowing that I am almost alive, my eyes
turning towards the window, a piece of sky, blue
as Joanie's summer eyes, the lithe limbs of a tree
swaying in the breeze, the tender dance of spring. The wanting
to arrive somewhere unencumbered, the yearning to walk
into another life of my own making—but
who made that other life, the one I no longer want—
who made that life *if not me?*

               I remember all the old
dreams. Of going to school naked, the shame of it, how
I tried to hide from the laughing world when there was no
hiding. I lived in variations of that dream: always
barefoot, the useless effort to hide my dirty feet. And I was left—
always, always shaking with that interminable fear. Dreams
are old gods that never die. They live in memory—and memory
is all they need to grow their choking vines.

How do I write another dream?

To be a tree. Each year, leaves to shade the earth.

              Here I am again looking at a sky
that carries only what it needs. It longs for nothing and I
am left yearning for a blue that I can never touch.

The night has come again. I am as weary as the war-torn
world. I must write another dream before I sleep. I must
write another dream before the dream writes me.

The Perfect Scene of Forgiveness

I begin to write a story—though I have no story in my head. But

I must have one, if I am writing it:

> He is sitting in a chair, drinking coffee. He is thinking of a scene in his past. He wants to go back and change the scene—and make it better. He never got his lines right. That is what he tells himself. He makes up intelligent and insightful remarks and places them on his own lips. That is what he should have said. But then he stops. He starts to rewrite the lines of the man he was speaking to. He tries to rewrite his reactions. But he cannot rewrite those lines. They are not his to rewrite. This is the problem with living. He is not a character in a novel. He cannot go back and change it any way he pleases. Characters in novels are articulate and consistent. But that is not the way he lives his life.

There is no changing what has been said.

There is no changing what has *not* been said.

There is only forgiveness.

I smile at the story. Is it a story? Where is the plot? I think this has something to do with my dream. I woke up saying *I'm sorry I'm sorry I'm sorry.*

I don't feel forgiven.

I don't want to go to a priest and tell him all my sins. It's a well-meaning sacrament but it doesn't change a goddamned thing. It doesn't fix a life.

I don't feel forgiven.

Let me analyze myself: the characters in my novels say all the perfect things I want to say. If I can't rewrite my own life, then I can rewrite somebody else's.
This is how I spend my days.

I wonder if all the roads in my head have something to do with escaping the life
I have made. What a strange way to put it. Does one make a life? Or does one live it?

I want to live it—this life that is mine.

The night has disappeared into the morning's perfect sky.

The plants are leaning into the sun.

My door leading to the balcony is open.

I can hear myself waking to the beauty of the day.

What We Photograph

All this is to say that in life everything is connected: your pain and your
imagination, which perhaps can help you forget reality. It's a way of
showing how you connect what you live with what you dream, and what
you dream with what you do, and this is what remains on paper…
                                                        —*Graciela Iturbide*

We are all photographers. Every day, I get a picture
courtesy of the internet. Photographs of friends, their children,
their dogs, the aftermath of a snowstorm or a hurricane, *I*
survived! I survived! The gala in New York I missed because I
had an appointment with a back surgeon. *We missed you, missed*
you, missed you. We are always in search of the lost or perfect
moment. The first thing children learn to do is pose. We place
those poses in a frame and whisper *I was there. I was really there.*
Once I was young and alive. The art of the already dead.

            There! On the corner of El Paso Street
and River! On the third floor balcony! Tiny white,
blinking lights surround a hand-painted sign that reads: *Imagine.*
The winter sun is setting and the aura of the dusk
in the calm and breezeless evening makes the world appear
as if it is about to catch on fire. Is it God who holds the match?
Or is it the hope and rage of the poor? We are afraid of rage.
We should be more afraid of hope. I think it's me who holds
the match. Sometimes, I swear I could light the whole world
on fire—and join in the dance of the flames. I'm trying not
to think of my skin on fire. I'm trying not to think of the pain.
My camera is at home. Not that I need one—not today—
though I hang on to it for emergencies. You never know
when you might need a camera. The perfect-moment psychology is
impossible to abandon. *Was I there? Was I really there?*
            For a time, I sit in my truck and whisper *imagine.*

I try not to think of John Lennon. I try not to think of his last
thought as he feels a strange bullet rip though his skin. I sit
long enough to spell out the word I-M-A-G-I-N-E. My body
is a book filled with scenes like these. I sometimes turn to them
in moments when my dreams threaten to swoop down on me.
I can switch scenes in an instant—a talent I developed as a boy.
There are days when I feel like a sparrow about to be snatched
up by a falcon in mid-air. Dreams have talons that can rip
your skin like paper. In this, they are like bullets. I am in love
with sparrows. They are small and common and exist in every
part of the world. There are sparrows in China and in France
and in England—and in the deserts of Arizona. They are like
Mexicans. What would the world do without sparrows and
Mexicans? What would the world do without cameras?

I am staring at a sky
burdened with the weight of hundreds of birds in a photograph
taken by Graciela Iturbide. The birds are circling a cemetery
in Dolores Hidalgo, Mexico. Someone has died. Someone is
always dying. Especially in Mexico. On another page, there is
a dead man lying on a path. The corpse is still dressed, pants,
shoes, but the vultures have pecked away his flesh. I want to know
why he was left lying there. I want to know whose uncle
this is. Maybe there are worse things than to become food
for hungry vultures. The wind was blowing hard last night. I
listened for hours. Even though the presence of the wind is
undeniable and lives in one of those dark corners in my body, it
remains unphotographable. I have accumulated too many dark and
empty corners. Someday, I dream they will be flooded
with light.

There are nights when gusts rise up
in me, gusts that mean to kill. I'm not ready to die. Too many
photographs left to take. I love the old photographs, the way
they translate the world into grays and blacks and whites.

That's funny. I would die without color. The New Mexico sky
ruined my vision. There is no logic to what the eye sees and loves.

                                                     I saw a man in his forties.
Sitting. Reading the newspaper. He did not know how perfect
he was in that sacred moment, his face half in the light—the
other half in an unfathomable shadow. I took that photograph
home and studied it. Who needs a camera? I have no idea
why my eye lands on certain things and why it wants to stay there
forever. I was waiting at a stop light. An old man with a cane
was crossing the street, hunched over, now he could only see the
ground. Does he ever see the sky? I would rather die.
And following him, a young man on a bicycle. He was singing.
I wondered about the song. *Imagine*. John Lennon. How beautiful to
sing. I do not believe there is such a thing as a sad song. Any
song at all helps the singer to survive. Have you ever heard a
dog howling out his grief? This is the sound of pain. It is not the
sound of despair. Today, I am going to walk around
with my camera in my hand. I dreamed barbed wire and birds.
I dreamed a sky full of rainclouds. I am going in search
of my dreams. I am again in search of that perfect moment.
How pedestrian. I am as common as everyone else. Rejoice!
Maybe the perfect moment is already alive somewhere inside me.
Maybe I am full of light. Maybe I am full of darkness. I don't care
about the pain. I don't care what my eyes fall in love with—
                                So long as they fall in love.

Salvation

Someone was trying to find me and I had no
desire to be found. I kept moving from place to place looking
for a country that would offer me asylum but it was raining. Raining
and raining and raining. And I had no umbrella. The weather is
always changing and I'm never prepared. On certain days it feels
like even the sun is looking for me just so it can
spit on my face. How to keep chaos at bay? What if what is
supposed to happen already happened—and I missed it. I am
not always present in this life I am living.

I should be in love with myself by now.
But hell, the world has too many solipsists already. Most
of them are in Congress and are telling me how I feel—not
me specifically but me as part of the *American people*. Since
they—the congressmen—are representing me so well there
is no real need for me to represent myself. Maybe they know
what I know: self-representation is a form of insanity. I am
being saved from myself. The truth is, I have never believed
everything I was thinking. Look, I'm busy with that list in my
head. *I forgot to pay that traffic ticket. Where is my book bag? Where's the
fucking cell phone?*

Something *is* supposed to
happen. Maybe it's happening right now. On Facebook. I do not
understand what is meant by *living* but I am beginning to believe
that it is related to the word *dying*. Maybe I'll do some of that today.
A little dying never killed anyone. Dying is fine—but dead?—well,
that's another thing altogether. Maybe today, I'll begin to learn
to spell *Salvation*—and learn too that it isn't something that's
supposed to happen after I'm dead.

Imagining the Universe of the Self

We are, each of us, functions of how we imagine ourselves and of how others imagine us, and, looking back, there are these discrete tracks of memory: the times when our lives are most sharply defined in relation to others' ideas of us, and the more private times when we are freer to imagine ourselves.
—Philip Gourevitch

Boyhood was a prison. I kept waiting for someone to let me out of my cell. All that time, misspent, letting all those disapproving eyes keep me in chains. There is this question of happiness. Some people have never known what it feels like to pursue it. I think of that young man who grew up in Chicago, who has never known another country, who wants to be a musician but he has discovered he is an "illegal." He worries, he hides. He says food doesn't taste good anymore. He wants to learn. He wants to taste. He wants to be happy.

Americans. We're a happy lot. We export happiness. The free market. That's what makes us so happy. Never mind that it's killing us. We sell houses to people who can't pay for them. We pretend the earth is dying of natural causes. We keep drilling. We are engaged in a scientific study. We want to find out exactly how much oil it takes to turn the Gulf of Mexico into a wasteland. The ocean, too, can become a desert. When we finish conducting our experiment, we can look at each other and be happy. Some people are never happy. Some people would climb a tree to be unhappy. They would sit on the highest branch and yell out their unhappiness to all the passersby. How many men and women stay in unhappy marriages? The Defense of Marriage Act. Now that should make us happy. Keeping men from marrying men. Keeping

women from marrying women. That will make us really happy.
How's your marriage doing? Is it making you happy? How many
people expect someone else to make them happy? Why should
someone else be doing all the work?

                  I always hear my mother's voice
telling me: "It doesn't matter what you do so long as you're
happy." No pressure. Just be happy. Moving out of the house
made me happy. But that kind of happiness only lasted so
long. Then the bills came in. I wouldn't be happy being a
mathematician. I wouldn't be happy working on Wall Street
or picking oranges in Florida. I should have been a therapist.
I'd be happier. But maybe not. Dealing with all those unhappy
people. I would have probably fallen in love with most of my
patients. That would have made me really unhappy. But then
again there's so much beauty in the pain of living that I want it
all to go on forever. It's true, I'm in love with the image of a god
dying on a crucifix. Most believers prefer the cross without a
real corpus. They skip the pain and move directly to the joy of
resurrection. I envy that kind of happy.

                  Some people think: *After retirement I'll be happy.*
Usually, they just die. Unhappy. Some people were happy when
they were in high school. Some people were happy when
they were in college. That kind of nostalgia makes you unhappy
the rest of your life. Some people are only happy when they're
pissed off. Pissed off is the new happy. Some people think that
only the young are happy. I know a lot of miserable young
people. Once, I asked my students what they knew about love.
One young man said: "I don't know shit about love." That made
me smile. If I smile a lot, does that mean I'm happy? What
is the correlation between laughing and happiness? There is
a scientist in this world who knows the answer. You wonder
if he's happy. If you laugh at people all the time, it can be a

sign that you're just plain mean. Or that you're a misanthrope. Misanthropes are never happy. They have small imaginations. They can't imagine decency. They can't imagine tenderness. They only have angry sex. Some people are always happy. They're annoying. They, too, have small imaginations. Imagine a man being tortured in the name of a beautiful ideal. Imagine all the people who have died—alone and ignored—and all because we were too busy pursuing happiness.

Manhood can be a prison too. It's a harsher penitentiary than the one I lived in when I was a boy. But it doesn't have to be this way. Why can't I be happy?

Smoking pot makes some people happy. These people are mostly unhappy. Most people are unhappy in their jobs. Including poets. I know poets who redefine morose. They're suspicious of happy people. They only listen to Billie Holiday and Tom Waits. But how can you *not* be happy sitting around all day writing poems? But there's that thing about having to spend time with yourself. So now we get to it. The whole frightening and complicated issue of spending time in the universe of the self. Don't look to the mystics. They were so afraid of being alone that they turned God into a lover. Sometimes I wish I could do that. Maybe I resent the mystics for their brilliant imaginations.

Looking back, it was me who kept me in chains. I wasn't born Black in the age of lynchings. I wasn't born a Jew in the age of the Nazis. I was called a few names. *Joto Queer Faggot.* I was born poor and speaking another language, but still I was surrounded by the beautiful rumors of happiness being whispered all around me. A lot of gringos thought I was inferior. I sometimes looked at myself through their eyes. I believed them. Is that their fault? In the end, I remained free enough to pursue happiness. No matter what vocation I was pursuing, I was always wanting others to imagine who I was. I trusted their eyes more than I trusted my own. I have finally escaped all my prisons. I am running my hands over my naked, imperfect body, memorizing all my scars with my trembling fingers. I have run out of excuses. I have given up all my public selves. At last I am beginning to live in a more private time. I am imagining. I am imagining myself. I am imagining myself a happy, happy man.

ONE DAY

Again I am summoned
to walk in the eternal fields of the dead. The bones
rise up, refusing to remain silent in the ground.
They are bringing me news of the day. They are
pointing out the position of the sun on the day
they were killed. I am drowning in the cloudburst
of the voices that are falling from the sky. This
is the only rain I know. Neither the journalists,
nor the photographers, nor the poets can raise them
back to life. Their lives are not a book for me to write.

One day, an angel will arrive
to lead me into paradise. I will send the angel away.
I never spoke the words I meant to speak. That silence
will be the only peace that I deserve. *I will send
that angel away*. I will refuse to surrender
to the theology of an afterlife. For me, there are
only hands that hunger for touch. For me
.there are only faces that look out with expectation.
I could use the word hope.

I am dreaming of Juárez.
I am dreaming of the river that separates my country
from the country of my ancestors. The river is flowing
with the waters of spring and it is no longer dry.
I am diving into the waters of innocence.
I am swimming toward another man who is calling
out my name. When we meet in that imaginary space

between his country and mine, his skin feels like

the desert sands. His kisses taste like the rain.

Ars Poetica

I'm wondering—
    let me stop myself here. Let me take
    a deep breath.
If only I could wonder at the wonder of it all.
I love Frank O'Hara and I may be sentimental
but I know romantic banalaties when I see them.
I stopped buying Hallmark cards when I was
ten. Already I was on my way to reading James Baldwin
and Dalton Trumbo. The Hardy Boys didn't do it
for me. Dick and Jane? Really? The image of a blue-eyed
resurrected Christ in a white robe offends me.
The beauty and generosity of the Christian myth
is one thing—blatant Aryan fantasies masquerading
as faith are something else altogether. I detest
Christian pornography. Give me the crucified
God begging to know why he was forsaken.
That's the kind of love I can understand. Suffering
and death aren't steps you can skip. I have better
things to do with my time than strip the corpus
from the cross. Iconography matters more
than we think. Even atheists know that. There are
days I want to believe that resurrection is me
sitting in a dive bar having a shot of tequila, a guy
with tattoos glancing over at me. It doesn't take
an analyst to figure out where that little piece
of theology comes from. Experience isn't always
a good teacher. Euphoric memory is the product
of a rearranged brain. I won't bore you with
the details of years of medical research. Anyway,
you won't believe me. Addicts are notoriously
unreliable—though what would the literary

world do without unreliable narrators? I woke up
one morning, wandering up and down the streets
of downtown El Paso. You can't learn from
something you don't remember. I had no
idea what I'd been up to all night. I have a few
theories. One thing's for certain, whatever
I'd been doing all night was not something I'd ever
bring up in polite company—though I've sworn off
having conversations with anyone who has
an obsessive relationship with the word polite.
Some people walk around all day, looking for reasons
to be offended. When they run into me, they've found
a reason to live another day. And some people don't
even have to drink or do drugs to experience
blackouts. What do you call a willful erasure
of history? Spending what is left of your imagination
re-enacting the Civil War—each day hoping
for a different outcome? Some people call that
a harmless hobby. I have another name
for that kind of behavior. While we're on the topic
of wondering, I'm wondering how I haven't lost
my mind. Not so fast—the jury's still sifting through
the evidence. Do juries have blackouts?
It's a lot of work to wonder at the wonders
of the universe—especially when planet earth
is being run by idiots pretending to be
theologians. Books will always be holier
than the people who read them. Are we all
sitting around, waiting to be stunned by poetic
language? Does a well-enjambed line turn heads
when it walks into the room? I used to live
in the words I wrote down on the page—which
made me a little crazy in the bedroom. Edit
the word *little* from that last line. I don't
take the phrase *mad with desire* lightly. That's

not a cliché—that's called playing Russian
roulette with your body.

Sometimes I just
want to sit and write about birds. If only I could
figure out the notes they were singing. Among
the things I've never learned: how to read
music. Maybe that's because I have no talent.
Look, I don't need to understand the physics
of notes to cry in the middle of a song. Is it the singer
who rips those tears from me? The seductive
melancholy in the melody? The voice that trembles
in its own suffering, desperately trying *not* to sound
desperate as it attempts to pull out all the weeds
that have overrun the garden? There has to be
room on the ground for corn. For tomatoes
and the lilacs to grow. I grew up on a farm.
I know something about weeds that take
advantage of the situation. Weeds will do anything
to survive. They're squatters hustling out
a living. I've been a hustler for years. I hustled
for anything I could get. I'm not talking about
my body here. I'm talking about my heart.
I'm so screwed. What the hell? If hustling for anything
that resembles love is what it takes to survive
then what's all the fuss about? I've broken
a few hearts here and there, *but I've never
actually killed anyone.* Sending the troops
out in the name of something we can't name—
that's insanity. That's hustling to the nth degree.
We'll make those fuckers love us one way
or another. Let's place hitting a meth pipe
in perspective. Does looking down at prostitutes
make you feel better? So it's come to that: *better
you than me* passes for morality. Listen, if I don't
survive, then how do I arrive at the phase called

living? It's become obvious to me that I am a great
admirer of weeds. That doesn't mean I've forgotten
the taste of a freshly picked tomato from the garden.

There are plenty of things in the world
to cry about. An obsession with tears and birds
won't save me, and it doesn't qualify as a vocation.
There's no money in it. You know, that thing called
survival. Ever try living without money? Let me know
how that worked out for you. Lately, I've been wondering
about salvation. I'm not talking about what happens
when I take my final breath. I'm gay. No one has to
tell me I'm going to hell. I already know that.
I'm talking about what I'm going to do today.
I'm wondering who I can call on the phone
just to tell them that I've fallen in love. With
the birds. With my own tears.   Sadness
doesn't live here anymore. I've put up a sign:
No loitering. Move along. Don't worry about
being homeless. I know plenty of people
who'll take you in.   I'm going to take
a shower now. I'm going to feel the warmth
of the water and concentrate on the feel
of the soap on my skin. Among my prized
possessions is a really soft towel. I can't say
I really know where I'm going with all this.
I'm going to hop on my truck. And just drive.

The Taste of Water

No despair in the driver's voice. Faith
is a word that clings to him. *We have lost a generation
to cartels and corruption. We have thrown our sons
away.* On the road to the Juárez airport, he asks me

where I'm headed. Being a driver has taught him
to believe in destinations. I smile with the simple
answer of a seasoned traveler: *México, la capital*. No
need to get into the dark details of journeys
that follow journeys that follow journeys. If
every human body is a nation, where does the capital
reside? The mind? The heart? The hungers
and desires of the flesh that find their way out
of imposed incarcerations? Don't drink and drive
and just say no. This is your brain on crack. There are
those who can't live by a motto or a rule or a law.
Ever been stopped by a cop? Did you feel safe
and protected? The word criminal isn't what
it used to be. What do I know? I should be in
jail. Instead, I'm walking around free. I'm thinking
about banishing that word from my vocabulary. Ever lived
in the prison of alcohol? I didn't even have to be
arrested. Thou shalt not kill. Let's hang that one
on the courtroom wall as we administer the death
penalty. Matthew, born in Pittsburgh, twenty-three
years old, a soldier, just back from Iraq, parked
his Chevy Silverado, took one last look at the night
sky, and shot himself with a .40 caliber handgun. He
had become the enemy in a private civil war. Pain
is a country that has no allies and no respect
for borders. The only passport you need is a gun

or a drug to move from one place to another. We
are always arming ourselves with the wrong
weapons. Unless, of course, the Beatles were right:
Happiness *is* a warm gun. The President of Uganda
signed a bill into law, prison for life for the crime
of making love to another man. What price
would I pay to touch another man? Would I die
to hold his hand? To die for a cause—is that any way
to live? I'm a drug addict. Details at eleven. And though
I no longer use, there was something living
inside me that wanted to die. I could tell you stories
about this country and an underground
economy that you know exists but don't want
to see. It all lands in our banks. Do you want
a loan? Arrest the dealer on the corner. Don't
make me fucking laugh. I quit smoking cigarettes—
twenty years later I started again. Then quit again. Then
started again. Addiction is not a phase. One night
I met crack and fell in love—the first of a long
succession of lovers. You think this is hyperbole?
You want subtlety? Read Hemingway. Just remember
he took a rifle and placed it in his mouth. I wonder
at the cool taste of metal on the tongue. We go looking
for what is missing. "I," the therapist says, "say
I." Which is to say, don't include everybody else
in your shit. I'm sticking with *we*. Either we're all
in this together or *we're not*. First, I had to translate
this whole thing about being Mexican. And what is
a Chicano anyway? Where is that essay I wrote? Then
I turned my attention to translating the whole
gay thing. If I hear the word *preference* one more time
I'm going to kick someone's ass. I may be a kind of
scrivener, but I'm not Bartelby. And now I'm translating
addiction. I never needed to read a book to become
an expert. I don't have the disposition of a translator.
The thrill of being a native informant has left

the building. I'm learning to smile and wave bon voyage
to all the ships that have sailed. I'm not a passenger—not
anymore.

I'm staying home. I don't feel
left behind. There was a time when I couldn't imagine
a life without alcohol or drugs. Which was a sure sign
that my imagination was even more limited than my
vocabulary. Yes, *amor*, there *are* ghosts hovering
all about me just as there are ghosts of headless men
haunting the streets of Juárez. If Juárez can survive—
then so can I.

Now, nothing comes between me and the sleep
I need to rest. I don't miss the panic of searching
for my wallet, of running out the door—the truck?
Is it still there? I don't miss the walks of shame. I love
the sleeping and the waking, the walking down
the street. Sidewalks and trees and Sam Smith singing
to a love he couldn't keep. Our songs remain long after
we have sent the lovers away.

This morning I woke. I took a clear
glass in my steady hand and filled it up with water
from the tap. I felt the smooth glass on my lips.
And drank. To wake to a dawn. And drink. Water.
I've changed my mind. I do want to be a translator.
To spend my days learning how to translate
the taste of water.

Easter Sunday 2015
(Again) for Carlos

Is it
       the weather that's changed
or something else? Thunder, lightning,
snow, tornadoes. Every season
offers its own apocalypse. I have known death
in summer. Green leaves shredded in the pelting
hail. Ruined crops and broken windows
in the house. I have made love during
thunderstorms, tasted the rain on the lips
of a stranger wandering the streets. I lived
in a season called thirst—and drank. I drank
and drank until I broke and lived in the echoes
of the breaking. I have felt the addict angry
stares that followed me from the waking into nights
that left me sleepless and shivering in a cold
no morning sun could warm. This: a rage
in a man's eyes, hardly disguised, no hint
of tenderness, touch and desire having divorced
the heart. To wake each day to the turbulence.
To wake each day to the savage shame. No
angel can take away the pain. What makes
a man a man? To return and return and return
to the same questions that rot like onions
in the abandoned fields of spring. To live
in that stench.   To return
and return and return to the ravaging routines
and rituals of want and revenge. All that's left
is a wasted body feeding on itself—and a voice
dissipating in the drought *When did I start to die?*

Now this: It's as if I'd never seen you. I study
your smile, tentative, and watch your face
in wonder. Your hurt subsides like a tide in a calming
sea. Even the waters of the earth have learned
the lesson of the letting go. A river loves the water
that it can never keep. The Easter season, quiet
and slow to arrive. Winter leaves reluctantly. To be
done with the cold. To be done with regret. To be
done with the grieving. To walk away from all
the graves. Faith does not belong to those
who've lived no Lent. There is no empty tomb
without a death. The letting go. The letting go.

I've learned the limits of my art. A heart can*not* be
placed in the still life of this page. What and who
you were and who and what you are—and what
you did. I thought I knew.   Forgive
my restless mind and the you that it imagined.

You live beyond the prison of my thoughts.
There are no words to name the wars you've fought.

Carlos, where is all that hurt? Where did it go?
Where did all the wounded waters flow?
          To the place where the sky meets the sea.
          To the place where the sky meets the sea.

          This then:
a man who's died as many times as me
has earned—   I can't survive on the nostalgia
of an Adam and an Eve. I don't pine for Paradise. But
I still cling to Resurrection.
I am the most reluctant of believers.
There is nothing left to do—except—of course—
to live. And then there's this:

There is no sacrifice so great that can make a stone of my
heart.

And finally this: I see you walking

down a road. I am walking on the same road.
I will look for you.
I will look for you. God
has no face but yours. God
has no face but mine.

YOU LEAVE A MESSAGE IN THE MIDDLE OF THE NIGHT
for Tony

The spring winds, a hint of cool, are dying down.
I am thinking of you. The evening sky
is pale and thirsty, the bougainvillea struggling
to bloom. I hate catching colds when
the days are edging toward summer. To think
this season once meant bare feet and innocence.
I am thinking this: You. Tony. I see you standing
outside the bar, a cigarette on your lips, the nodding,
knowing smile. *Baby, hey babe, hey babe.* You were
an illness that made me vulnerable, sentimental,
that made me want to give everything. When
there's nothing left to give, at last you're free. Just
when I stopped uttering your name, just when
I thought the illness—why did you call? Why
did I answer the phone? It's the way you speak
my name—expectant—and then wait for me
to speak. And then your laugh that's all boy
and charm, the way I imagine your eyes that are
nothing but hurt. My head feels as though it's made
of the cotton I picked as a boy. I would work
the whole day, picking and picking, my hands
scarred and scratched, my back aching, my lips
cursing my circumstance. I am sitting where
you used to sit, making a list of hurts, looking out
into the street, searching for traces of your steps.
I sweep and gather your cigarette butts, throw
them away, wash my hands—then wash
and wash again until I scrub the smell of ash
and nicotine away.
           The time for loving cigarettes is gone.

You loved beer
and crack. You loved heroin, ecstasy, the sad music
of the bars. You said you loved me too. I am
thinking of the night I met you. Late October
night, the breeze as soft as your black eyes. You took
my hand and placed it on your chest. You were
so hungry for trouble. I was so hungry
for anything that resembled love. My finger
tracing the tattoos on your chest, I dreamed
of living in the prison of your arms. But I refused
to live in the prison of your deadly nights. I
can't survive without the morning
light. I wake to the sound of sparrows
and the need to write a word and see its beauty
on the page. I repeat this again and again:
You're a man, not an illness. Tattoos and prison.
Novels and poems. *A bird can love a fish but they can't
live in your apartment.* You called again last night
and left a message that was meant
to wound. The worst winds are the ones

that gust through an angry heart.
I whispered your name in the dark.

You said: *I want to know what you meant when
you said I love you.* I said: I love you. I meant I love you.

You said: *I want to know what you meant when
you said goodbye.* I said: Goodbye. I meant goodbye.

My finger tracing the tattoos on your chest,
I whisper your name in the dark.

He. You. I.

       This August day, I rise
to a morning rain, a summer song running through
my head. I'd lost them once, the songs I'd loved.
I hadn't even noticed they were gone. They're back now.
Theo gathered them and gave them back to me. He lives
in the Bronx and knows everything there is to know
about rain and lost songs. He knows about flowers
and everything there is to know about the laughing heart.
Some days the living is easy. The lost days, the forgotten
hours, the ravaging nights have left. For now. No one
knows if they'll come back. There was nothing left
for them to take. It was time for them to leave. And time

for me to wake—   I've looked
at me as if I wasn't me. And I became a him. And
I became a you. I've lived my days and weeks in fragments,
shards of mirrors I shattered, not wanting to see
my own reflection. Now I'm gathering the pieces
like crumbs strewn on the road, hoping
to find my way back to Jerusalem.

          I carry these memories: a man blocking
the sidewalk in front of Jimmy's Market who's looking up
at me, *All I need's a quarter to get home*. Tony is sitting on
the sidewalk in front of the Mesa Inn, his head hanging low,
his eyes so dead that all the sadness is gone. Carlos is standing
in the distance texting on his phone with his crooked
finger as he carries the eternal question. I ache
to hand him an answer, all the while knowing
there is none. I cannot give what I do not have to give.
Gustavo is dancing on the bar, his hips gyrating, hustling

for attention. Nobody hustles for cash. Not Gustavo, not
Tony. Not me. Not Carlos. Gustavo is beckoning:
Come be with me. He's dead now. The dying will never
cease. I am sitting across from where I used to live.
The house is empty. The lights are off. Gatsby's green light
of hope has been snuffed out. I am in a march in Juárez,
all the surviving young around me. They are jumping
up and down singing *el que no brinca es chota*. I am
jumping with them. I am chanting with them. I am watching
a Tanzanian boy holding a banana leaf over his head
as the rain falls softly on the East African ground. If
only his innocence could save me. I am twenty-five
years old—and discovering the world. I am walking
into la Basilica de la Santa Cruz in el *Valle de los caidos*
and wondering how many of Franco's enemies perished
building this monument of shame. I am in the Louvre
standing in front of Gericault's *Raft of the Medusa*, tears
running down my face. If only art could tame the cities
of the world. I am knocking at the door of a homeless
shelter for men in Kilburn and staring into the dark
eyes of an Indian nun who wants to know
if I have the wrong address. Marcel Marceau is walking
across a London stage. His wordless art, a strange
condemnation: it is we who are the clowns. I am
standing in Trafalgar Square as the cold and endless
rain comes pouring down. I am warming myself in
Joanie's eyes that are as blue as a desert sky. An umbrella
and her eyes. That is all I need. Somewhere, there
is always a summer.   There is a dead man
lying on the campus of the university and I am staring
down at his body. No one knows who he is and how
he died. I am sitting in a wicker chair, smoking
my last cigarette.

How many quarters does it take to get home?

Every day now, I drive
forty-two miles up and down the interstate. They are repairing
all the bridges. They are repairing all the roads. I have never
been a good driver. I brake and swerve. But here I am
driving. Here I am, this morning, listening to songs. Here
I am singing as if God had given me a voice. I don't
give a damn if I'm singing off key. I'm singing. No one can
kill this song inside me. Not even me. The clouds
are feeding the hungry soil with rain. I could live forever
in this tender hour. He is here with me. You are
here with me.

And here I am—with me. All of us. Here.

After Great Pain

This is the Hour of Lead—
Remembered, if outlived,
As Freezing persons, recollect the Snow—
First—Chill—then Stupor—then the letting go—
                                    —Emily Dickinson

When I was a boy, I became enamored of studying the sky. Maybe I found eternity there. Maybe I was looking for God. Maybe I saw a mystery and a beauty there that I couldn't name. Through the comings and goings of my life, I have often turned my eyes upwards, the same question entering into my waking mind: *What would you do without the air?* I don't know where that question came from. I don't even know why it has kept coming back. But always this question has been important to me—sometimes urgently so.

I have a need to understand what my life is and why it matters. I remain a mystery to myself. I live my life in contradictions that cannot easily be reconciled and I have often lived my life in extremes. I was once a Catholic priest. I was once married to a woman for fifteen years. And I am now living my life as an openly gay man. No matter where I found myself, and no matter how good or disappointing my life appeared, there was always an emptiness in me that needed to be filled: a gnawing, a wanting, a needing to experience that undefinable something more. There was some insatiable desire in me to reach for something that I had never imagined. If I was always an ambitious writer, I was even more ambitious as a man, a man who wanted to live in opposition to what people considered normal.

I wasn't ambitious in the usual ways: I didn't want a big house in a fancy neighborhood. I didn't want or need or seek respectability or money or power. None of those things captured my imagination. I wanted to experience life on the edge. I had no idea how strong that desire was until the moment a man, a stranger, sat next to me in a bar, kissed me and wanted to know if I had ever tried crack. I didn't flinch. I didn't hesitate. I responded out of pure instinct. I was fifty-four years old. It was as if something in me recognized how long I'd lived my life in fear—and it seemed that I had been given an opportunity to be free of that word.

I wanted to live.

I have always been profoundly in love with life. Looking back, I think it's something of a miracle that I survived a journey that can only be called self-destructive. When I attempt to examine my own life objectively (an oxymoron if there ever was one), I see one thing that I can say is absolutely true about myself: I have always turned to art to give order to all the riots that run rampant in my heart. I've used my perceptions, experiences, and memories filtered through my own emotions and poured them into a container called poetry.

Art requires discipline. Addiction necessarily implies the abandonment of discipline. I moved between having no control over myself to taking back control by turning to art, whether it was through painting, poetry and/or the writing of fiction. My own acts of creation have always done battle with the part of myself that was hell-bent on self-destruction. The making of art revealed to me a self that was almost pure—despite the fact that at one point or another I violated almost every moral principal I ever held. I would like to believe that there is an indestructible purity to human existence despite the fact that there is so little purity left in the life I have lived.

I've spent five years attempting to write this impossible book. These poems colonized so many of my days and nights that it felt as if they owned and operated me. The thought never crossed my mind to abandon my project—perhaps because I felt the stakes were so high. And in any case, I couldn't have let this collection of poems go simply because I have never been very good at letting go of things and people I love. And although it may seem strange to admit, I came to love the writing of this book. Or maybe it became yet another addiction. But I always thought of addictions as a kind of love. Love can be a dangerous thing and men like me are not afraid of danger. Perhaps danger is a kind of love I have too often embraced.

I remained fierce in trying to get at something essential that involved both my life and my art. Each poem I wrote came no closer to getting me where I wanted to go—though in truth I had no idea where I wanted to go—except to arrive at that mythical place we refer to as home. I somehow felt as though I had crossed some kind of border illegally and was desperately trying to find documentation in order not to be deported. Perhaps I was trying to build an argument as to why I should be allowed to reenter a life that I had decided to abandon. No one who feels themselves to be living in exile can ever know peace. Exile is a kind of hell where the word *belonging* has no influence, no efficacy, no power.

I spent hours, days, weeks, months—months that turned into years, living in a self-imposed exile attempting to make connections between things I had lived or seen or dreamed, connections between the waking and the sleeping where the sleeping felt as if it were a place of acute awareness and the waking felt like an eternal nightmare from which I would never wake.

I became chronically obsessed with making connections between the city I lived in and the nation I lived in and the country that was my body. Everything was connected, must be connected. I put my energies into collecting all the fragments, all the clues, all the data I found scattered among the roads I traveled, trying to make myself whole through the poems I was writing, knowing all the while that many of the pieces fit together because I made them fit together. I wanted so much to understand what I was doing and the language of recovery fell short, placing me into a paradigm that seemed not to say what I wanted to say.

It is an impossible task to decipher the mysteries of the self. Parts of the self are unknowable, unfathomable, and out of reach. Desire can be explained but why it stubbornly seeks to quench its thirst in a place where there is no water is something that I can never, will never, fully comprehend. What I *did* comprehend was that the profound experience of desire—a desire I had never before experienced—left me in a chaos I never knew existed.

Of course, there are always intersections between art and life. Tracing those intersections with any kind of exactitude proves to be a difficult, if impossible, task. I wrote these poems not so much out of a need to create but out of a need to survive. I spent my days and nights attempting to map the journey of my own heart struggling against itself and I became a cartographer of a dark and unknown country. The world of shadows provided little light. Have you ever met the shadow people? I hope you never do.

I remember sitting at a gay bar in downtown El Paso. It was around ten o'clock at night. I was on my cell phone. That was the last thing I remembered before coming to consciousness at five o'clock in the morning walking through the deserted streets of downtown El Paso. It was as if I appeared on the scene out of nowhere. I will never know what I did that night.

Later, I came to think that amnesia was preferable to remembering. It was painful to remember. Addicts don't want to feel their own pain. Pain is a messenger that brings us a truth we often cannot bear to hear. Living in a meth-induced paradise proved to be not only impossible but deadly. The euphoria of meth swept the pain away but no mood-altering substance is ever as strong as the pain it is medicating. And when the pain returned, it returned with a vengeance. It seemed to me that the word suffering had replaced the word living. I thought of Descartes whose investigation led him to his *cogito ergo sum*. To think, for him, was proof of his own existence. I wanted desperately to be numb. But I just kept on feeling. My emotional life was the only evidence I had as proof that I was not yet dead.

I knew I was alive because I was in pain.

This manuscript has gone through innumerable revisions. Revision after revision after revision, searching for an exactitude I did not believe in. There were moments I felt so emotionally exhausted, my labor came to a halt. I was paralyzed. Immobile. I could not grow paradise on the fields where I labored. The soil was spent, had succumbed to the many years of drought. Drought, that was a word I was familiar with.

I was a man who had lived in drought for so long that what I desired most was rain. But the rain never came.

Poetry became the rain I turned to. It was a rain of my own creation. Inexplicably, I who had so vehemently scoffed at those who romanticized about poetry and its efficacy, came to believe that poetry was something pure—and I was anything but. Poetry became a path of transcendence. Poetry brought a sense of order to a life lived carelessly. If I spent my days in apocalyptic nights, then poetry became a normalcy I desperately clung to.

If I have often been careless with my life, I'd like to think that I have not been as careless with my art.

I dislike emotional exhibitionism. I dislike, even more, emotional anorexia. Becoming a man has been a harsh and difficult journey. One of my limitations as a poet is that my work is not fundamentally an intellectual endeavor. I want my work to have emotional weight, emotional honesty—and always I want to say something I have never said before. I have never really written about what it felt like for me to love. To love another man. The most difficult decision was to include the poems I wrote for Carlos. In truth, I wrote them for me. Carlos was never my lover. Our friendship defies easy categorizations—and I will leave it at that. But I do feel compelled to say this: you will not find Carlos, the man, anywhere in these poems. You will only find my own yearnings and confusions.

⁜

I am sixty-two years old and the remembrances of the life I have lived have no systematic organization. There may be a kind of chronology to my memories—but they are chaotic at best. My life is not a timeline nor is my life the accuumlation of the things I have done. There may be such a thing as facts but what of it? The facts of my life are of little use to me since, as it turns out, I use facts merely as tools to interpret or misinterpret who and what I am. This occurs to me just now: when memories decide to walk into my living room, there is no door with a lock that is capable of keeping those memories out.

To add another complication to the complications: my memories are unreliable narrators. I have often placed too much weight on a moment that ought not to have had any weight at all. I filter facts to create an organized narrative that keeps the chaos of my life at bay. My life is disordered, chaotic, sometimes apocalyptic, living some of my life in my body and very often living my life in my head. I have paid too much attention to my own wounds and paid too little attention to how I have survived those wounds. But even a man who has little need of certainties needs a semblance of order to survive. Without any order at all, I would go stark raving mad. I've had a glimpse of that madness—and wish never to see its face ever again. Perhaps that is where my need to create comes from. I am a poet, a novelist, a short story writer—and a painter. I have relied on my art to give me order and to unravel the mysteries of my own identity. No therapist could take the place of the poems I need to write.

I'd like to say that the day brings what the day brings. There is a large and overwhelming truth to this. It is a confession that I am not in control, and that control is nothing more than a necessary illusion. Though the passing of time and the rising and the setting of the sun are part of the workings of the universe, they are movements that do not need my presence—though it intends no insult. The simple matter is that the universe does not need my existence. It has no need of me at all. Ah, finally I arrive at the heart of the matter of these poems.

Today, I am alive.

My life is simpler now. There are simple rhythms to my days that feel like the almost silent waters of a pond. The noise of the roaring, raging rivers feels like a distant memory. The writing of these poems is an attempt to map out a journey that I was stupid enough (or perhaps brave enough) to embark on. It is a crude map of my own survival. I have at least learned to own my mistakes without having to live my life in regret. Guilt and shame may give evidence to the fact that I have a conscience, but those words have lived too long in me and they have proved to be a destructive force.

When I say that writing has saved my life, I mean that *writing has saved my life*.

I sat on the steps of the fire escape this morning. The air was cool from an unexpected rain the night before. I sipped on my coffee. I had a cigarette. I tried to imagine another life. I found myself smiling. Why would I want anything more than I have now? I have found and lost and found and lost and found and lost myself so many times that now, exhausted, I have finally arrived at a place that is as close to home as I have ever known. How could I ever want another life?

ACKNOWLEDGMENTS

A poet once said that the basest of all human traits was ingratitude. I would very much hate to be accused of having such a trait. And yet uttering words of gratitude, I feel a sense of inadequacy. Words may well have the power to offer salvation, but even words have their limitations. How can you truly thank the friends who loved you back to the land of the living? Their names are written in the book of saints: My sister, Gloria (who is and will always remain, my person), Jaime and Noelia Esparza, Teri Garcia, Lynn Coyle and Paco Dominguez, Theo Nieves, Virginia Navarro, Hector and Annie Pedregon, Barbara DuMond, Monica Ortiz Urribe, Phillip Conners, Stefanie Block, Alvaro Uribarri, Enrique Moreno, Bobby and Lee Byrd, Eddie Castenada, Patty Moosbrugger, Chris Hornsby, Chris Bailey and Jamie Enchinton de Bailey, Tom Star, Michael Rosenbaum, Raquel Urban, Michael Fedewa, Angela Kocherga, Alfredo Cochardo, Pat Witherspoon, Laura and Jim Nicosia, and Carlos Daniel Sainz.

My gratitude can never equal what you have given.

OTHER POETRY COLLECTIONS BY
BENJAMIN ALIRE SÁENZ

Calendar of Dust
1991

Dark and Perfect Angels
1996

Que linda la brisa
(with James Drake and Jimmy Santiago Baca)
2001

Elegies in Blue
2002

Dreaming the End of War
2006

The Book of What Remains
2010